SINGAPORE PERSPECTIVES 2017
What If?

SINGAPORE PERSPECTIVES 2017
What If?

Edited by
Gillian Koh
Debbie Soon
Institute of Policy Studies, Singapore

Published by

World Scientific Publishing Co. Pte. Ltd.
5 Toh Tuck Link, Singapore 596224
USA office: 27 Warren Street, Suite 401-402, Hackensack, NJ 07601
UK office: 57 Shelton Street, Covent Garden, London WC2H 9HE

British Library Cataloguing-in-Publication Data
A catalogue record for this book is available from the British Library.

SINGAPORE PERSPECTIVES 2017
What If?

Copyright © 2018 by World Scientific Publishing Co. Pte. Ltd.

All rights reserved. This book, or parts thereof, may not be reproduced in any form or by any means, electronic or mechanical, including photocopying, recording or any information storage and retrieval system now known or to be invented, without written permission from the publisher.

For photocopying of material in this volume, please pay a copying fee through the Copyright Clearance Center, Inc., 222 Rosewood Drive, Danvers, MA 01923, USA. In this case, permission to photocopy is not required from the publisher.

ISBN 978-981-3224-74-2 (pbk)

For any available supplementary material, please visit
http://www.worldscientific.com/worldscibooks/10.1142/10566#t=suppl

Desk Editor: Sandhya Venkatesh

Contents

Preface ix
Janadas Devan

Acknowledgements xv

Introduction 1
Gillian Koh and Debbie Soon

SECTION I
Looking Out

Chapter 1 19
What if the Nation-State is No Longer the Key Organisational Unit of the International Community?
Wang Gungwu

Chapter 2 31
What if Globalisation Fails?
Khong Cho-Oon

Chapter 3 37
What if Singapore Has to Choose Between China and the United States?
Joseph Liow

SECTION II
Looking In

Chapter 4   51
What if Non-Economic Indicators Become the Measure of a Country's Progress?
Jeremy Au

Chapter 5   61
What if Singapore Fails to Become a Creative and Innovative Nation?
Aaron Maniam

Chapter 6   67
What if Singapore Fails to Sustain Itself as a Vibrant, Cosmopolitan "Global City"?
Amanda Chong

SECTION III
Looking Across

Chapter 7   77
What if We Ignore Race and Religion?
Norman Vasu and Pravin Prakash

Chapter 8   93
What if We Cease to Accept Immigrants?
Mariam Jaafar

Chapter 9   105
What if the Family is No Longer the Fundamental Building Block of Society?
Thang Leng Leng

SECTION IV
Looking Ahead

Chapter 10   121
What if Singapore Becomes a Two- or Multi-Party System?
Ong Ye Kung

Chapter 11   127
The Real Question Behind "What if Singapore Becomes a Two- or Multi-Party System?"
Ho Kwon Ping

About the Contributors   135

Preface

JANADAS DEVAN

We usually have one-word themes for Singapore Perspectives: "Inequality" in 2012; "Governance" in 2013; "Differences"; "Choices" and "We" in the following years.

The theme of this year's conference was somewhat more prolix — "What If?" — two words, plus a question mark.

It was designed to set us thinking of possibilities — or perhaps impossibilities: What might be, what might have been, what could be.

But before we consider these possibilities, it might be instructive to locate what is — what has always been, what should not change, what shall always be.

Is there a permanent substratum to our existence as a nation-state that will persist no matter what else changes?

I would suggest that there is — and it would be foolish of us to ignore it. "Things and actions are what they are, and their consequences will be what they will be: Why then should we seek to be deceived?" wrote Bishop Joseph Butler (cited in Berlin, 1996, p. 1).

First, we cannot deceive ourselves about our geography, our location: This is a small island — mostly hard granite — in the middle of Southeast Asia, not Europe, not off the coasts of the Americas, not next to Antarctica.

This is one of the most religiously diverse regions in the world, with almost half of us Muslim and the rest a rich polyglot of Buddhist, Christian, Hindu, Taoist, Confucian, diverse folk religionists, and goodness knows what else.

This religious diversity is accompanied by staggering cultural, ethnic, political and historical diversities.

For the dense forests of the region, its ubiquitous waterways, made difficult the emergence of vast, unifying empires of the sort that came into being in the great plains and river systems of the Eurasian landmass. It is possible thus to speak of a European or Chinese or Indian civilisation; not so a Southeast Asian civilisation. This region has always been a borderland — always diverse, always in-between, always at the crossroads of other vast civilisations — as some of the geographical terms that persist to this day indicate: *Indo-nesia, Indo-China.*

As an aside, I might remark that Sir Stamford Raffles did not found here for the first time an open port; he came to Singapore because it was right smack in the middle of a borderland region that was, by definition almost, always already open.

That porosity also ensured that Southeast Asia's encounters with modernity differed dramatically from country to country. Six European powers colonised various parts of this region at different times — the Portuguese, the Dutch, the British, the French, the American, the Spanish; not forgetting the brutal Japanese interregnum.

As each of these metropolitan empires receded, they left behind a multiplicity of political, legal and educational systems. Our different modernities accentuated the diversities that were already endemic in this borderland.

And the diversity of our region is replicated too in our own diversity; the diversity without, mirrored in the diversity within. That is the other thing that will persist no matter what else changes. I need not dwell on this, for we are accustomed to acknowledging almost every day our racial, linguistic and religious diversities. I would only add that though we have travelled far these past five decades to become "one united people, regardless of race, language or religion," as we state in our National Pledge, there are new diversities that we have to deal with — among other things, diversities arising from immigration and the diversities arising from income inequality.

Let me dwell on something else that will persist no matter what else changes — or to be more precise, what I think (and hope) will persist: Namely, the fact that Singapore is a country as well as a city. We do not always keep this foremost in our minds — we forget — but Singapore is a city that happens also to be a country; a country that has no country — as in "country-side" — outside the city. Or to put it differently, there is no country beyond this city; this city is all the country that we have.

I am sure all of you have encountered the puzzlement of immigration officers in foreign countries when you write two or more times "Singapore" to specify the city, state and country of your birth or address or embarkation. Singapore, Singapore, Singapore — like a needle on a broken record stuck on the same groove. But despite the repetition, I am not sure we are fully conscious of what it means to have a country that encompasses no more than its only city. Actually, the fact that this city is all the country that we have informs every facet of our existence.

Let me try to illustrate this as economically as I can:

One, Singapore is the only city in the world that has a military and a foreign service too. London does not have a navy; we do. Tokyo does not have an air force; we do. Shanghai does not have an army or armoured personnel carriers, for that matter; we do.

Two, all of Singapore's gateways — its port, its airport — have to be located within the city. You cannot put Changi Airport, for instance, somewhere out in the boondocks, a couple or so hours outside the city — like Narita or Dulles or Suvarnabhumi or Heathrow or KLIA — for the simple reason Singapore does not have a boondock. You disembark at our gateways and you are already within the city; not so much as a drawbridge or a moat separates the city walls from the outside.

Three, unusual among global cities, Singapore has a sizeable manufacturing base — almost 20 percent of our gross domestic product. There are a number of reasons why this should be so but one is because we are a city as well as a country. If we were to have a purely service economy — like London or New York or other global cities, with high-paying jobs in finance and banking at one end and low-paying jobs flipping hamburgers and providing *in-situ* services at the other — our income inequalities would be far worse. Indeed, our Gini coefficient is already high when compared to other countries. When compared to other global cities, we are considerably better off — in large part because we have a substantial manufacturing base providing a range of jobs in the middle.

Now, guess how much land — physical space — do these three activities, which this city has to undertake because it is also a country, occupy: military (for training, airbases, naval bases); gateways (airport, port); and manufacturing?

Whenever I ask this question of students or civil servants, the guesses vary from 15 percent to 25 percent. The correct answer is 42 to 43 percent. That's right, nearly half of this not considerable little red dot, and I have not included the land that we have to devote to — according to the Land Use Plan of June 2013 — water reservoirs (5 percent), housing (17 percent), roads and rail (13 percent), parks and nature reserves (9 percent), and all the other accoutrements of civilised existence (Ministry of National Development, 2013, p. 5).

You see, Singapore is a most unlikely country. There is no other city of this size in the world that is also a country. That is why our founding fathers, every one of them, began their political lives believing Singapore, a city, could not survive on its own, that it had to be joined to a hinterland, Malaya; and believing that, they fought for Merger, only to be ejected from Malaysia after less than two years, to become a country with no countryside, a city-state with no hinterland. That Singapore should exist — as a city and a country — is a miracle.

"What if?", we ask, imagining a series of possibilities: What if the nation-state is no longer the key organising unit of the international community? What if globalisation fails? What if Singapore fails to sustain itself as a vibrant, cosmopolitan "global city"?

In a way, we are inviting you to imagine what if the conditions of Singapore's existence — as of now — no longer prevail. But actually the fact that we exist is in itself proof the impossible is possible.

What does it take to sustain this miracle — this impossibility? Let me rehearse a few factors, none of which should come as a surprise, but they are worth identifying in any case, to ground our speculations:

One, as suggested by how just three functions that we undertake because we are both a city and a country occupy so much space, this place has to be an exceptionally and intricately well-organised organism — or it cannot exist at all.

Two, Singapore cannot be exceptional without having an exceptional government — an exceptional government that can plan decades ahead, take long-term decisions, and sustain purposeful action over long stretches of time.

You cannot get a Marina Bay without such planning. You cannot convert almost the entire island into a water catchment area without this capacity for sustained long-term action.

You cannot keep this miraculous organism — a country in a city — alive without such a government.

We saw some years ago what happens when the government's capacity to plan ahead falters: the trains became crowded, the waiting times for new flats stretched for years, there were not enough hospital beds. Actually, when compared to failures of governance elsewhere, these were stumbles. The ruling party paid a price nevertheless in the 2011 General Election, and many (including not a few baffled foreigners) said Singaporeans were an exceptionally spoilt people.

On the contrary, I think Singaporeans were correct to expect their government to always be exceptional. Forget about high ministerial salaries and transactional politics: Singapore cannot exist without exceptional government. You cannot have *laissez-faire* government in Singapore, let alone second-rate government. *Laissez-faire* would have meant staying in Malaysia. Singaporeans should always expect the best of their government — which ultimately means they must expect the best of themselves.

Which leads me to my final point: Singapore cannot have exceptional government unless Singaporeans too are exceptional. This might sound an awfully cloying cliché but it happens to be true. If ever we become so silly as to elect buffoons into office; if ever our politics becomes so toxic as to allow nativist, neo-fascist, populists into power, we are unlikely to have a second chance, a redo; we would be finished.

This has nothing to do with one-party dominant or two-party systems — the final topic of discussion. It is a given, I believe, that our politics will inevitably become more contested — for the simple reason that our society is diverse, the challenges and issues we face are complex, and an increasingly better educated population open to the world is bound to have different views on public policy. All that is well and good.

The challenge is maintaining exceptional government — capable of that sustained, long-term planning and action, without which this city cannot be a country — even as our people become more diverse and our politics more contested. Can that be done? It will not be easy.

Things and actions are what they are, and their consequences will be what they will be: Why then should we seek to be deceived?

But don't forget: Most people elsewhere in other countries saw things as they were, and wondered "Why?" But the 1965 generation of Singaporeans dreamt of things that never were, and said: "Why not?"

What if?

Well, why not?

REFERENCES

Berlin, I. (1996). *Karl Marx: His life and environment.* New York: Oxford University Press.

Ministry of National Development. (2013, January). A high quality living environment for all Singaporeans: Land use plan to support Singapore's future population. Retrieved from: https://www.mnd.gov.sg/landuseplan/e-book/files/assets/basic-html/index.html#page1.

Acknowledgements

IPS is grateful to the following institutions
for their support of Singapore Perspectives 2017.

TEMASEK

Introduction

GILLIAN KOH AND DEBBIE SOON[1]

THE THEMES — UNDERSTANDING AND RESPONDING TO CHANGE

The Institute of Policy Studies (IPS) held its annual flagship conference, Singapore Perspectives (SP) in 2017 on January 23. The theme of SP2017 was "What If?", with the intent of inviting speakers and participants to consider counterfactual scenarios of Singapore within the spheres of international relations, economics, society and politics for the year 2065 when the country celebrates the 100th anniversary of its independence.

Singapore has seen remarkable development in its first 50 years as a sovereign nation-state. We felt, as part of the organising team of the 2017 conference, that we should use the occasion to re-examine some of the country's key governing institutions, systems and values that are in place and often taken for granted. The challenge we set ourselves was to consider potential game-changing scenarios around these and ask what would happen if they were modified or abandoned in response to internal and external changes.

As we usually plan each year's conference about nine months before the day, in April 2016 as we drafted this conference concept, we could not have imagined how quickly the world would be set on a different tilt by January 2017.

---

[1] We wish to thank Tan Min-Wei, Research Assistant at the Institute of Policy Studies as well as Leong Wenshan for all their kind assistance in the process of publishing this book.

On June 23, 2016, by a slim margin of 3.8 percentage points, citizens of the United Kingdom (UK) voted for the country to withdraw from the European Union (EU). After all that had been done to keep Greece in the EU and the European Project alive prior to that, the outcome was seen as a vote against globalisation and the liberal concept of economic regionalism built around free trade, movement of labour and investment; of social and labour standards for inclusion; and the sense of shared prosperity and security further undergirded by its membership of the North Atlantic Treaty Organization.

Then on November 8, 2016, another political earthquake struck — the populist, nationalist political neophyte Donald Trump was elected by the Americans to be their 45th President. Gauging from Trump's narrative and stated policy agenda, the vote for him sustained the anti-globalisation momentum of the June decision on the other side of the Atlantic.

Significant proportions of citizens in these bastions of the Western liberal democratic and capitalist systems or the Washington Consensus had said that they were no longer sure they were benefitting sufficiently from these to vote for the status quo. Given how immigration, income insecurity, wage disparities and the recognition of moral hazard of selecting members of the existing political elites back into power were at the heart of the ambivalence driving the votes in the UK and the United States (US), those debates did not escape the attention of Singaporeans. Voters were seeking to re-balance their national politics and were making a global impact with their choices.

Closer to home, the region was on its hunches on July 12, 2016, when the Permanent Court of Arbitration at the International Court of Justice in The Hague delivered its judgment in a case that the Philippines brought before it to establish its sovereignty over territories and resources in the West Philippine Sea also claimed by China. The latter, which had refused to participate in the action, said it would not acknowledge the ruling that covered strategic outcrops, reefs and atolls it had built military facilities on and over which it had rights to on the basis of a historical unilaterally declared "Nine-Dash Line Map". Given the rules of the United Nations Convention on the Law of the Sea (UNCLOS), China's lack of participation did not deprive the court of its jurisdiction.

The worry, of course, was not just with how the Chinese would respond to the Philippines but also with the possible spillover effects to the former's relations with other countries in the region. China would wonder if the decision would embolden those countries and its ultimate rival, the US, to pursue similar action. What pre-emptory action would China take?

Singapore, a non-claimant state, said it supported the peaceful resolution of maritime disputes according to universally recognised principles of international law without the use of threat or force. As a small state, Singapore said it fully supported the maintenance of a rules-based order that upholds and protects the rights and privileges of all states. It also stated that it supported the effort of the regional Association of Southeast Asian Nations (ASEAN) community to develop a legally-binding code of conduct in the South China Sea with China, first mooted in 1996. Since the Association's 10 members operate on the basis of ASEAN centrality, this means that the interests of the group prevail over the approach and interests of individual member states. ASEAN's stance is to set up the legal framework and protocol for managing activities in the disputed waters and find modalities for joint development, mutual benefit and prosperity for all claimant states.

This position is different from that of China's which has consistently indicated that it prefers to settle all disputes on a bilateral basis. The divergence in approach has been apparent since the Obama administration in the US stated in 2010 that it was in its national interest to ensure freedom of navigation and open access to what it called Asia's maritime commons. It said that international law should be respected in the South China Sea and noted that China had made overreaching and aggressive claims to the area. The US has since regularly updated the international community of what appears to be military and logistical facilities that the Chinese are building on the reefs and islands in the region.

Will there come a time when an ascendant and assertive China pressures or seduces Southeast Asian countries to stand on its side than on what it would perceive as the US' side? The geostrategic value of different forms of regionalism will be tested. It will raise the question of whether small states like Singapore can viably protect their sovereignty on their own with the backstop of international law for a sense of security, or whether it is only by being openly identified as being in the camp of one of these two powers that paradoxically, small states can achieve some autonomy? How will this outlook change if Trump's America means that the global geostrategic as well as economic order goes through a paradigm shift, rather than just a tilt?

When it comes to Singapore, however, we have always known that it is by being recognised as a successful economic hub and an exceptional country that we have been able to garner enough interest in our survival from the world's major powers. Singapore has also made a great deal of diplomatic investment in the international rule of law. Over the next 50 years, how will we ensure that we maintain our sovereignty and be that global city that is a key node in business and financial value chains? If the major countries of the world turn inwards to define their national interests more narrowly and abandon trade-facilitating regionalism, what can Singapore offer that will make us nonetheless relevant to them? Does Singapore also have other strong internal engines of wealth creation to power it forward under those changed circumstances?

In addition to our economic competitiveness, what has surely been integral to our attraction to the world or, our soft power, is our success in living with diversity — social and cultural difference. Part of what is driving the populist movements of the West, in addition to the terror threat that stems from the geopolitics of the Middle East and the attendant refugee crisis, is the sheer pushback against the cultural diversity that globalisation has brought with it through the liberal regime of labour flows and immigration.

Simply for its own sake of course, the Singapore governance system has invested in ensuring that multiculturalism works. Singaporeans are grappling with the question of whether the future should be where cultural difference is explicitly recognised and actively accommodated as one model, or de-emphasised so that all are treated as equal without consideration given to anyone's race, language, or religion, as another model.

Yet another level of social complexity in Singapore arises from the fact that we are an ageing society that has depended on the traditional concept of family as the first line of social support. How tenable is this if family size shrinks and the older dependents live longer, or aspire to live independently? Will this be a cause of intergenerational conflict — placing the state in the middle of a debate on whose burden it will be to care for the elderly in Singapore? What of the strategy of allowing for calibrated immigration to mitigate these demographic trends? What are the long-term trade-offs of an even more restrictive approach to that?

In the end, whether it is foreign policy, economic or social frameworks, ever greater demands will be placed on the quality of political leadership. As governance orthodoxies and assumptions are re-written, citizens will think of progress, success and good governance in more multi-dimensional ways than before. How will we respond?

We are certainly glad that the conference discussions seemed so relevant to our audience by the time the January 2017 conference rolled around, but of course no one is celebrating the fact that we find ourselves in a world that has become far more volatile, uncertain, complex and ambiguous, and in particular, so ambivalent about globalisation and the liberal world order that we had prospered under. We see the international community prevaricating on upholding the system of international law and angry citizens out in force to say that they do not believe the liberal order has served them well.

While we seemed ambitious to stretch out the time horizon in our considerations to the year 2065, we also hoped that it would allow contributors in the room to re-imagine what Singapore might be, two generations from now. We received insights and ideas that are nonetheless immediately accessible and also applicable for navigating the changing world we face today.

So what did the speakers at the conference, whose papers are reproduced in this volume, have to say?

LOOKING OUT — STRATEGIC CHOICES IN GEOPOLITICS

In the first section we call "Looking Out", we focus on geopolitics. Historian Wang Gungwu has a sobering message for us. Many of us may have imagined that it was the sense of self-determination of nations that had been the driving force behind the formation of nation-states as far back as 1648 with the conclusion of the Treaty of Westphalia. Our confidence is that this is a strong, deep-set, ideational foundation to the international system. Professor Wang explains however that it is only a recent development of the post-Second World War era. What is the truer impulse of human civilisation has been reasserting itself forcefully — might is right. As history has shown, boundaries, especially of the small states and minor powers in the 17th century, were established after larger powers were tired of fighting over them; a *modus vivendi* is arrived at for a season until the power balance shifts.

As a small state that has worked hard to realise the ASEAN community, our takeaway is that neither ASEAN nor Singapore can afford to have any illusions that international law, regional treaties and conventions of conduct will prevail when the geostrategic balance between the US and China starts to shift. There is no room for complacency; of operating under the assumption that other individual Southeast Asian states will always define their sovereignty and strategic interests by their place in ASEAN as they interact with China and the US.

Joseph Liow, the international relations scholar who recently returned from his perch at the Brookings Institution in Washington DC as the Lee Kuan Yew Chair in Southeast Asia Studies, analyses this most important geopolitical relationship as it stands today. He argues that while Trump has suggested that the US is prepared to recede from the region and the Chinese have become ever more assertive, both powers have invested in a bilateral relationship that is deeply intertwined and interdependent in many ways. As such, open conflict between the US and China is unlikely, he argues.

If however, for various reasons that Professor Liow spells out, the strategic balance between the two powers changes, or if it begins to appear that there is an implicit arrangement to carve out spheres of influence between them, Singapore may be confronted with the scenario it has worked hard to avoid — having to choose between two superpowers.

If so, Professor Liow offers five key points for consideration: first, that Singapore must choose its position based on interests, not countries; second, the understanding must be that Singapore will not tolerate any interference in domestic politics; third, that Singapore must be wary of the signal our actions may send to neighbours about our resolve to stand our ground; fourth, there are other powers of consequence in the region that Singapore should strengthen our ties with; and fifth, a move by us may affect ASEAN's cohesion and its ability to secure "much needed autonomy from the centrifugal forces of great power politics."

Political scientist and Shell futurist, Khong Cho-Oon (who spoke before Professor Liow at the conference,) provides the larger backdrop for the convulsions that the world is going through today to help us imagine the likely scenarios the world will face in the next decades. His position is that globalisation is an inexorable force, especially in the technological sense of it. What is uncertain is the specific nature of it.

The first direction that globalisation can take is where there is a forceful resurgence of nationalism and national competition. Illiberal political systems will be at play in a scenario called "Mountains". The other scenario is called

Introduction

"Oceans" where people power and vigorous civil society challenge governments and traditional ruling elites. This is a diffused form of globalisation with alternative paradigms of and therefore debates on how common challenges to humanity can be dealt with. Each of these scenarios has its attending costs and opportunities.

The worry is about how many transboundary challenges like climate change and demographic shifts can be managed without cooperation among the major powers of the world; without the sort of liberal order that we had before Trump and Brexit. Ultimately, a small state like Singapore that has benefitted in so many ways from the globalisation of science, technology, trade, investment and talent as well as the rule of law and respect for national sovereignty must hope that that order does not change drastically. The question of climate change alone is so critical to small island states like ours that we must depend on effective global cooperation among states and international civil society to manage it. Singapore's omni-directional efforts at securing such arrangements globally, regionally and bilaterally, therefore, must continue in this age of disruption.

LOOKING IN — APPROACHES TO BECOMING A GLOBAL FORCE OF INNOVATION

The second section is titled "Looking In", to explore the areas that Singapore most certainly has control over in shaping its future. This is not just about the country's soft power and its ability to maintain its image as an exceptional country, but about nourishing the sense of who we are and our creative and entrepreneurial talent; firing-up our creative resources for its own sake. What would Singaporeans consider "progress"? How would we achieve it? How important is being a "vibrant, cosmopolitan global city" in that vision of progress?

Social entrepreneur Jeremy Au was asked how he would define "progress" for Singapore — "What if non-economic indicators become the measure of a country's progress?" Clearly, the usual measure of a country's gross domestic product (GDP), that is, the value of everything that it produces, is the simplest but inadequate measure of life satisfaction and happiness that Singaporeans want, he argues. Au suggests that we adopt a more holistic "Singapore Development Index" that is centred on achieving what is encapsulated in the National Pledge — unity, racial harmony, democracy, justice, equality, happiness, prosperity, and progress. So, how have we done thus far?

The Gallup World Poll is an annual survey of just over 1,000 respondents in each country, and Au taps on this to illustrate how the Singapore Development Index could work. Comparing data from the 2016 poll with the average scores from polls of the past years, the responses on unity, harmony, democracy, justice and equality were all above the average and some had risen slightly that year. It was the ratings for happiness, prosperity and progress that were lower than the average score and had slid downwards in recent years. To end, Au appeals for more thought around a holistic measure like the one discussed so that academics, policymakers and leaders across all sectors of Singapore can discuss the effort that must be made to "unleash the extraordinary potential that is within," he says.

Public servant and poet Aaron Maniam was invited to discuss what might happen if we fail to be a creative and innovative nation; if we are unable to harness our creative potential. He structured his comments in three sections — why we might fail; if that would matter; and how we can avoid that. The most critical point that he makes is that we might fail because we think and speak of this process of fostering creativity and innovation as an input-output, mechanistic process that can be set off through to extrinsic stimulus. This, he says, is an incomplete understanding of the creative process as it leaves out the role of inspiration, of what is non-linear, sometimes whimsical and driven by what is within and intrinsic to the creator. To fail means that we may be less able to adapt to unprecedented situations or opportunities and more importantly, that we will have to be content with mediocrity.

How can we successfully unleash creativity and innovation in Singapore? While there is a lot of the mundane as well as discipline in the process of creation and innovation, it is helpful to perceive the creative process as a "biological" one that results from living, breathing, adapting and non-linear leaps of exploration and change. The second point Mr Maniam makes is that it should be motivated by the concept of the "gift" that one brings that is of great, oftentimes intangible worth. Also, to be open to "surprise, opportunities and serendipity." There is a real need to layer upon or even replace the previous approaches that emphasised just the economistic, deterministic and mechanistic with these other ideas about the creative process.

Lawyer and poet Amanda Chong places similar emphasis on the question of motivation in her offering on the question of "what if Singapore fails to sustain itself as a vibrant, cosmopolitan global city?" She makes the distinction between wanting Singapore to be a colourful, artistic, creative economic dynamo from the "outside-in" — a government strategy to attract money and global talent to Singapore — and doing it from the "inside-out" simply because being all those things and growing the arts in Singapore has value in itself. It is an expression of what Singaporeans are and want for themselves.

She says "the arts can be a vital way of constructing Singapore as a global city from the 'inside-out'", of becoming a mature, self-confident nation. How will this happen? The arts allows for expression of the full complexity of truth and helps us avoid reductionist approaches to understanding it; it provides a way to recognise our common humanity and helps people identify with one another. It "resolves" Singapore's "crisis of story" as it is a way to host, elicit and express the multiplicity of voices, to explore their inner worlds and interrogate the Singapore identity. Chong's is an inspirational vision of the arts that will "elevate our spirits and engage more deeply with the people around us." She adds:

> The arts is a critical space in which our collective thoughts about Singapore are renewed. It is a way that society reiterates the ideals that are precious to us and protests the ones which need to be remade. As Singapore moves on from the project of survival to the project of building a legacy, the arts is a crucial way of visioning the country as we yearn it to be....

What the contributors seek to express is their view that an authentic and probably sustainable way in which to be a vibrant nation and global city is for people to find their own voice and craft their own future. This is as much an organic effort as it is one that is facilitated by institutionalised structures and a gift that each citizen offers to himself, his community and country. In this way, it is the non-economic process of achieving deep human fulfilment that translates to or drives economic progress as a consequence. It is interesting that the contributors' convictions is that identity-making can translate to wealth generation in all senses of that term. What of the shape of Singapore society as that happens? This is addressed in the next section.

LOOKING ACROSS — THE SOCIAL CONTOURS OF THE SINGAPORE OF THE FUTURE

The third section is titled "Looking Across" which considers how Singapore society will evolve going forward. Chong, in the earlier section, refers to how the idea of Singapore's future especially as "global city" is associated with attracting foreign talent to our shores. While there has been a moderation of that strategy and more generally, the foreign labour policy, over recent years, in this section, we ask the implausible question: "What if we cease to accept immigrants?" This was a way for us to draw out a framework for thinking not only about the costs and benefits of the immigration policy for Singapore's future but also elicit further ideas about the social integration of foreigners.

Mariam Jaafar grapples with the issue by doing four things: First, she cites, as a positive vision, the economic value of immigrant entrepreneurs to the American economy — a 2013 National Venture Capitalist Association study, between 2006 and 2012, when immigrants started 33 percent of US venture-backed companies that went public. Second, she says that the immigration policy should be more adaptive. She discusses four scenarios of the socio-economic future of the country shaped by four drivers of change which are technological change, changes in the global economy, the social impact of the changes and the political climate in relation to economic development and finally, the role of labour. She proposes that ways be devised to receive signals of change that translate to experimentation in public policy and business strategy. Third, she urges that every effort be made to "elevate" the Singaporean core of the labour force which we know is being done now through firstly, heavy investments by the state in skills-training and education, and secondly, with the fair consideration framework that provides a mechanism for market-testing the need for foreign labour. Fourth, she argues that it is time to broaden the conversation about Singapore's future to include the views of foreigners so that they too can share their aspirations and find common interests with Singaporeans.

Immigration has and will continue to add social diversity to Singaporean society which itself is diverse and fosters its own level of hybridity. While non-citizens comprise 40 percent of Singapore's total population today, one in five marriages are between citizens of different ethnicities and four in 10 newly married Singaporeans have spouses of a different nationality (National Population and Talent Division, 2016, p. 4 and p. 11). Given that the basic framework for managing race in Singapore continues to be the Chinese-Malay-Indian-Others categories to ensure the inclusion of all Singaporeans in public programmes and political institutions, and that religious communities are recognised and protected from any insult or harm, we decided to ask if any of these frameworks should be changed and if so, how?

In Norman Vasu and Pravin Prakash's contribution, "What if we ignore race and religion?" we are invited to consider two alternative approaches to managing our diversity in the future. To begin with, the current approach is what is referred to as "hard multiculturalism" where the state intervenes to protect cultural differences given the assumption that first, racial identities are relatively immutable and second, that religious identity is always assumed to be deeply-held, where the beliefs of one group can conflict with another or even compete for loyalty to the state.

The first alternative approach is where race and religion cease to matter to the state — this is called "mild multiculturalism". Under this model, cultural diversity is deemed to belong completely in the private sphere. The public sphere of law, government, education, the market, and specifically, the labour market are reserved as a neutral spaces that are agnostic to race and religion. They think this system would be deemed too "quixotic", "utopian" and revolutionary.

The second possible approach is an evolutionary shift to a "Singapore-Plus" model where clear targets for social inclusion are set, say on the basis of ethnicity, so that educational attainment and the taking up of key occupations reflects the demographic distribution in the country. Vasu and Prakash conclude with the following vision:

> Singaporeans from different cultural backgrounds would be able to look at and, more importantly, experience Singaporean life as it is — a rainbow of phenotypic hues and religion, reflective of reality whatever the sphere of interaction; a place where one can be anything one strives for based on a system of culturally vigilant and sensitive meritocracy. Rather than ignoring race and religion, or viewing such a shift as being impractical, the current framework can

evolve to target structural issues to foster greater multicultural unity. Surely such an approach would be both pragmatic and satisfyingly Singaporean.

Since a key issue under the "Looking Across" theme has to do with social support, Associate Professor Thang Leng Leng was asked to consider: "What if the family is no longer the fundamental building block of society?" This is a critical question because the assumption now is that the family is the first line of defence when it comes to addressing social needs. There are, however, three key trends that could erode that assumption about intergenerational support and care provision. First, given the ultra-low fertility rates over the past decades and trends in family formation, there is likely to be a rise in single and one-generation households especially even as we age rapidly as a country. Who can the seniors depend on when they are in need? Second, the younger cohorts of Singaporeans are tired of the overtly-explicit message that family must care, a point reinforced legally through the Maintenance of Parents Act. Even if they desire to take care of their seniors, they may find that their long hours at work make that challenging. Third, based on survey data, many Singaporeans say they would prefer to live as independently as possible as they age. This is in good part because the respondents to the study worry if their children will be able to support them at all; they do not wish to be a burden to their families. The question then is what sort of living arrangements would suit them? Will specialised retirement villages work? How can we better prepare Singaporeans to age-in-place?

Thang cites other survey data that suggests that friends and neighbours are an invaluable source not only of social and emotional support but also of financial and instrumental support. This applies to residents in low-income rental flats too, especially among long-term residents within the same block of flats. This is one way to address the "shortfall" in care that may emerge in the future. As such, effort will be needed to nourish such ties through the design of the neighbourhood. Another source of invaluable support are pets and this is not just for the direct psychological effect on individual seniors but because pets also give occasion to owners to meet and interact with other owners. Again, these potentially generate valuable social ties. The question is whether the living environment of Singapore's growing group of seniors can be made pet-friendly. Finally, robots can help with practical functions but the technology also allows robots to engage with humans effectively. Thang urges us to work with the fact that the family is taking diverse forms and recognise that there is a need to try out different healthcare, financing and social frameworks to meet the needs and aspirations of our greying population, rather than rely on the orthodoxy that family must be the first and primary source of support.

LOOKING AHEAD — ENSURING GOOD GOVERNANCE, STRENGTHENING DELIBERATIVE DEMOCRACY

Ultimately, what all the earlier discussion boils down to is whether Singapore will continue to have a political and governance system that can be responsive to disruptive change as well as citizens' concerns and aspirations to make the strategic choices that the future will throw up. This is the issue that lies at the heart of the final section of the conference and book, titled "Looking Ahead". The current Minister for Education and Second Minister for Defence, Mr Ong Ye Kung, and Singaporean businessman and thought leader, Mr Ho Kwon Ping grapple with the question: "What if Singapore is a two- or multi-party system?" Both contributors recognise that this sought to elicit their views on whether the ruling People's Action Party (PAP) will maintain its one-party dominance with the bottom line concern: Will Singapore continue to have a responsive governance system that allows its people to be successful and the country to remain exceptional? If the PAP were to lose its dominance, why would that have happened; what would the implications be; what would it mean in terms of the quality of the social compact between the government and people; and what would the PAP have to do to avoid that fate, but more importantly, to continue to serve citizens well?

Somewhat contrary to the discussion in the preceding sections however, Minister Ong's view is that being small, the range of feasible policy options on any major issue for Singapore is not so large as to translate into a highly pluralistic political landscape. There are no widely diverse policy platforms that would all work well for the country and over which politicians and voters might fundamentally disagree.

If a majority of citizens were to vote against the PAP, this would suggest that a large fissure must have occurred between the PAP and voters. This scenario, Minister Ong argues, is likely to occur only if the PAP falls to three risks of long-term one-party dominance: first, complacency which means it is no longer responsive to the changing needs of society and people; second, elitism which means its policies seem only to reward a particular group and neglect the needs of the rest; and third, corruption such that the PAP will have lost the trust of the people.

Minister Ong says that such a scenario must mean that there will be rifts arising from partisanship in many social groups and institutions. The civil service will be tested the most for its ability to remain professional as it is called upon to replace policies it had helped to put in place previously should a different party come to power.

Taking a comparative view, Mr Ho highlights how the PAP does indeed have difficult odds to beat given that other one-party dominant systems have fallen into three traps: one, sclerotic policymaking as the policies and solutions that led the founding party to succeed in government become "sacred cows"; two, dynastic or nepotistic politics; and three, a culture of entitlement that leads to corruption. This list mirrors the risks mentioned by Minister Ong.

Mr Ho says he is sure that if at all, this decline will not happen for another 20 to 25 years because the imprint and influence of the current prime minister who is himself the son of the founding one, will still be strong.

He provides a prescription for the PAP to transcend those risks which is, first, for it to open itself to competition — internal competition for succession within the party which should not be about a contest among personalities but of ideas; and second, to welcome external competition afforded by allowing for a lively civil society that is facilitated by a much freer flow of information and views. He places his faith in citizen-driven watchdogs to ensure that falsehoods in the media are called out. Together, these will facilitate the emergence of a richer, more robust deliberative democracy that can protect the PAP and Singapore at large from dysfunction and decline.

CONCLUSION

Responsive governance that adapts to changes from within and without, improves the lives of citizens, allows for the creative flowering of their potential, keeps Singapore a vibrant economy and an exceptional nation, fully sovereign yet deeply engaged in the international system — this book raises the issues and provides the ideas to achieve that based on a realistic appreciation of the world as it is today and on some emergent trends. We hope that the challenging material here will inspire you to contribute proactively to the creation of Singapore circa 2065.

REFERENCES

National Population and Talent Division. (2016). Population in brief 2016. Retrieved from: https://www.nptd.gov.sg/PORTALS/0/HOMEPAGE/HIGHLIGHTS/population-in-brief-2016.pdf.

SECTION I

Looking Out

CHAPTER 1

What if the Nation-State is No Longer the Key Organisational Unit of the International Community?

WANG GUNGWU

I do not believe in the end of history. It was surprising how quickly the nation-state came to be seen during the last few decades as the key organisational unit of the international community. I will not, however, be surprised if that ceases to be the case. The flux of historical change is the norm, but the idea of progress arising from scientific and technological advances does not apply to units of political organisation. No such unit has remained unchanged or unchallenged for long. It is justified to ask what other kinds of units could take the nation-state's place.

Janadas Devan, the Director of the Institute of Policy Studies, responds to one part of the question in the Preface of this book when he describes the very exceptional position of Singapore. His account of its origins — the difficult roads taken to enable Singapore to survive and grow — provides an excellent snapshot of how conditional and incalculable the fate of each unit that calls itself a "nation-state" can be. If the "city-state" of Singapore is a "nation-state" and an exceptional one, one may well ask, what is a "nation-state"?

THE MYTHS ABOUT THE ORIGINS OF THE NATION-STATE AND INTERNATIONAL LAW

My instincts as a historian are aroused because the city-state that Mr Devan describes is closer to what had been an ancient institution. There have been city-states of various kinds, and some did survive for centuries. They have not had a happy history and teach us nothing about the origins of nation-states.

On the other hand, nation-states are taken as the norm by many today who assume that such states have always been around. In fact, the nation-state is a very new idea. It came into being under a special set of circumstances in Western Europe.

Most of my colleagues, the political scientists in particular, would say that the system of nation-states dates from the end of the Thirty Years' War with the Peace of Westphalia of 1648. If that is correct, the nation-state can be said to have begun in one corner of the world over 300 years ago.

However, the more I learn about what happened before and after Westphalia, the more I am convinced that it is a myth that the nation-state began to play any historic role from the 17th century. The nation-state, as an organising unit of the international community, certainly cannot be dated back to the treaties signed at that time. Why do I say that?

The treaties signed at the time were not between nation-states but by more than a hundred Catholic and Protestant polities of many different jurisdictions and sizes that had been involved in religious wars for decades, some to a greater extent than others. The main protagonists that fought themselves to a standstill had decided that they should stop killing one another and sit down to talk about achieving a lasting peace "among good Christians". After several years of discussions, the various rulers finally agreed that they should draw up borders between the aggressive combatant states. Each of these sovereign states would agree not to interfere in the affairs of the others.

The treaties were, on the one hand, between kingdoms and empires and, on the other, between them and a large number of princely states, imperial cities and imperial bishoprics. There was no such thing as the nation-state in their eyes. What made the agreements enduring was the fact that they shared a deeply rooted cultural heritage, one based on a common religion and a respect for juridical authority. Nevertheless, there was one state that was close to becoming what we now recognise as a nation-state. This was the Dutch Republic that had fought the Eighty Years' War to gain its independence from the Spanish empire. Many historians acknowledge that this was the first state that established itself as a union of people with one language, one religion and a shared anti-imperial history.

The great innovation at Westphalia, nonetheless, was the idea that the sovereignty of each state should be respected and no state should interfere in the affairs of another. It has since been argued that it was this principle that enabled nation-states to emerge eventually. It is certainly true that some of the small princely states in Central Europe began to have safe borders, and some did survive for a long time. It should be clear though that these treaties, based on agreements reached among the powerful empires and kingdoms of the time, had little to do with the rising tide of nationalism later in the 19th century, which saw the formation of most of the European nation-states.

Westphalia represented a high point in the Age of Empires. By that time, the Spanish maritime empire was already powerful, and the Portuguese empire in Brazil, Africa and South and Southeast Asia was the most extensive, being spread around the world on all the known continents. Several decades earlier, the British, French and Dutch had launched merchant companies that began building their rival empires in the Americas and had then launched their commercial empires in Africa and Asia. Outside Western and Central Europe, there was the Russian empire in the north spreading eastwards overland into Central Asia and reaching beyond Siberia to the Amur River and the Pacific Ocean. Towards Central Europe, the Islamic Ottoman empire had probed deep into European lands and controlled the southern shores of the Mediterranean. Other inheritors of the Mongol empire had conquered most of the Indian Subcontinent. China under its Manchu Qing dynasty was feeling its way westwards to check the advances of the Turkic and Russian empires.

In short, the treaties at Westphalia agreed to largely by the rulers of empires, kingdoms and princely states in Western and Central Europe were to stop incessant fighting within Europe itself. This gave the smaller polities among them a period of relative peace and security that enabled some to develop their respective local identities ultimately into a sense of nationhood. They benefited from the fact that the expanding empires had agreed to pursue their imperial interests elsewhere. However, it is one thing to say that the idea of sovereignty began in the 17th century but quite misleading to say that was when nation-states came about.

The second myth is that it was an evolving system of international law that made the nation-state the organisational unit of the international community. Modern ideas of international law are said to date back to Hugo Grotius, following his 1625 treatise, a few decades before the Westphalia treaties. Grotius sought to establish a set of rules that would enable empires like those of the Portuguese and the Dutch to minimise their rivalry and warfare in Asia, especially in the maritime Malay world. His treatise was well-argued and what he proposed was necessary. This had nothing to do with the rise of nation-states though. It became necessary primarily because the Portuguese were Catholic and the Dutch were Protestant. Unlike earlier disputes between the Spanish and the Portuguese, both Catholic empires, the Protestant Dutch could not, like the Spanish earlier on, resolve their differences with the Portuguese by appealing to the Pope.

Thus, Grotius provided the two sets of Christian powers with the idea of drawing up a set of rules to minimise conflict. Of course, it did not stop the Dutch from seizing Malacca from the Portuguese in 1641 when they had the power to do so. When interests between empires collided, international law meant little. That was so then and threatens to remain true today.

Similarly, as efforts to draw up rules of peace and war developed, wars between empires continued over larger areas of the globe and with increasing ferocity. That reached a climax with the Napoleonic Wars which came to an end in the early part of the 19th century. One of its results was that the British naval empire in the East won out totally against that of the French. Ironically, this has been regarded as a high point in the evolution of international law, with the treaties associated with the Congress of Vienna that was convened in 1814 ensuring that a peaceful era for Europe would last for several decades.

The various meetings that accompanied the Congress did work out more permanent understandings as to what sovereignty might mean for empires and the Great Powers, and what the law could and should allow. International law could also affirm principles as to why states should not invade each other and how they should behave towards one another. Some people would argue that it was only with such a set of international laws that small states could feel secure; and only with the existence of such law could nation-states become a key unit in the international community.

That is an acceptable proposition but it must be clear that this happened because it was also in the interest of the powerful empires to agree to it. International law was not designed with nation-states in mind but was really about minimising conflict between very powerful European empires. These empires were then free to use their military power to expand their respective empires in the rest of the world. For example, with better understanding among them, they could carve out different parts of Asia and Africa without resorting to war among themselves.

In any case, the countries that really mattered were the Great Powers led by the British national empire and supported by the equally nationalist French empire. Other kinds of empires, like the Austro-Hungarian, the Prussian and the Tsarist Russian, were not far behind. By the 1840s, it was understood that the civilisation undergirding the law of nations was Christian and only civilised nations could be regarded as equal sovereign states. The Islamic Ottoman empire was admitted only after agreeing to extra-territorial rights in what might be described as an unequal treaty. Later, under military pressure and the threat of war, the Qing dynastic empire in China and the Buddhist Siamese empire submitted to similar conditions of what was described as international law. Soon afterwards, American show of "Black Ships" power in Tokyo Bay brought the Japanese emperor to accept a similar kind of unequal treaty.

It was also in this context that the Qing empire was forced to conform to the standards of civilisation dictated by Britain and France. By those standards, neither the Qing empire nor the Republic of China after 1912 was recognised as being "civilised". As long as the Chinese republic was regarded as weak and divided, it was not treated as an equal, full member of the international community. Only by accepting extra-territoriality was Qing China conditionally recognised by the other empires. By so doing, it also allowed a number of smaller European states to obtain Most Favoured Nation status that, when added together, subjected the treaty zones of China to becoming virtual parts of large and small Western Christian empires.

Perhaps the most significant shift in international law at the beginning of the 20th century was the equal status given to the Japanese empire after its surprising defeat of Qing China and later the Russian empire in the East. Clearly the acquisition of wealth and victories against other powers were the key criteria of civilisation even when Japan was not a Christian country. Yet, the Japanese could not overcome the issue of racial equality when the League of Nations met in Versailles in 1919. At the insistence of Britain, American President Woodrow Wilson as chairman denied Japan's proposal for the Japanese to be treated as equals. The Versailles meeting proved to be a rude awakening for both China and Japan, the former surrendering German rights in Shandong to Japan and the latter failing to gain racial equality for its people.

In short, the international law that was seen as maturing during the 19th century was not only about how empires should behave but also about which empires were more equal than others. It managed to reduce conflicts among national empires like those of the British and the French overseas but that did not stop them from expanding at the expense of other states. In the end, that law could not help the states avert the wars within Europe itself. As a result, two very destructive so-called World Wars followed each other closely. Ironically, the most destructive result of these two wars was not the demise of the small nation-states that were emerging in Central and Eastern Europe, but the collapse of the huge British and French empires.

It was only after 1945 that the world saw the age of the territorial empires finally come to an end. With global de-colonisation supported by a liberal, capitalist United States (US) as well as an internationalist Soviet Union (USSR), we can, for the first time, talk about the beginnings of a world of nation-states. With the United Nations (UN) replacing the League of Nations in 1945, the idea of using the nation-state as the key organisational unit for the rest of the world may be said to have become conceivable.

What made that feasible were two global developments. The first began in Europe with the secularisation of the Christian states during the 19th century. By the 20th century, it was possible for international law to accept that non-Christian states could also be treated as civilised. This enabled the Western powers to take the next step and consider the idea that former colonies might eventually qualify to become sovereign nation-states, all equal in law.

The second development followed the first. At the end of the Second World War, superpower rivalry was between enemies divided by secular and materialist ideologies — the US with its liberal capitalism and the USSR leading the charge for internationalist socialism. This led to a deadly struggle to draw all nation-states, especially the newborn post-colonial ones, into one camp or the other. Here, the small states must be thankful to international law, especially where it provided valuable cover for the new nation-states to be built and helped some of them resist the pressures of the two superpowers.

THE POST-SECOND WORLD WAR LANDSCAPE OF THE NATION-STATE

I have turned to history to emphasise the fact that the nation-state became a key organisational unit for the world only very recently indeed. It was the UN that provided the structure which made that feasible. I recall how enthusiastic I was when I first learnt about its establishment in my final year at school in 1946. Later, at university, I was carried away by its promise and participated in the first meeting of the UN Students Association held in New Delhi in 1951. There, observing the new national pride of my fellow Indian students, I looked forward to the day when Malaya would become independent as a UN member state.

This was despite the fact that I felt disquiet that five countries were Permanent Members of Security Council and could act as super-states. When the UN rallied international forces to fight against invasion on the Korean peninsula in 1950, I was confident that we could count on the UN to ensure that small nation-states were safe from their big neighbours.

It turned out, however, not to be that simple. The Cold War led by the two superpowers lasted for more than four decades. When the USSR fell, the world was left with one superpower for some 25 years. The reality was that any powerful state could always find reasons to intervene in the affairs of smaller nation-states, not only in the new and poor ones in Africa and Asia but also in Eastern Europe.

In addition, the UN was helpless when some member-states were forcibly divided into two or more new states. We have seen how quickly Pakistan was divided into two. Then, the people of what could have been an obvious Korean nation-state have had to live ever since 1945 with what seems like an impossible dream. The unification of divided peoples has been possible but it was not something that the UN has enabled. At one end, we have the example of Vietnam reunified by a very bloody war that, unexpectedly, the US allowed the Vietnamese to win. At the other end, the reunification of Germany came about suddenly without any help from the UN.

It is in that context that we can see the reason for the "what if?" question that has been put to us.

I began by saying that Mr Devan rightly reminded us about the shifting borders around Malaysia that finally turned the parts of the British empire which use Malay as national language into three nation-states. For 20 years after the Second World War, there were no clear borders in most of this region. There has only been a more or less stable border since 1965. Singapore's neighbour had to fight very hard to make Indonesia the one country that it is today, not only against the Dutch who tried to hold on to parts of their empire but also against secessionist movements. Fortunately for Southeast Asia, all those efforts failed.

The survival of these states is not something that can, however, be taken for granted. The idea that once a nation-state gains its sovereignty anywhere, it will always be able to maintain it, has not been fully tested. The most glaring examples of how a "nation" can become several new nation-states can be seen from the collapse of the USSR, and the example that most surprised the whole world was the violent fragmentation of Yugoslavia. What kind of nation-state can turn into five different nation-states almost immediately after the death of its ruler?

That is a very cruel reminder that what is called the nation-state is still work-in-progress. There is hope that international law, the UN and all the institutions that the world has tried to support and strengthen for the last hundred years will succeed in protecting the nation-state ideal. The fact is there has been new thinking about global governance and about other kinds of organisational units to supplement or complement the nation-state.

ALTERNATIVES TO THE NATION-STATE

Is the nation-state the only organisational unit of the international community? Allow me to consider three other possible developments or arrangements. One is that some nation-states could set aside parts of their sovereignty and

The Nation-State and the International Community

pool their resources to form larger unions, as has been the case with the European Union (EU). A second possibility is that some nation-states might opt to break up into more comfortable and sustainable units, for example, the Czech and Slovak republics and, possibly, also a future Scotland and Catalonia. A third possibility is a move away from nation-states altogether, with a group of city-states looking to the example of the once-flourishing Hanseatic League of Northern Europe as a model for that.

Let me assume that, given changing attitudes towards the global promise of the UN vision, the nation-state is no longer seen as the key organisational unit of the international community. Leading the way in this approach are states in Western and Central Europe where nation-states have had a longer history than anywhere else. Soon after the Second World War, some of them decided that they had enough of the conflict among them and began to plan for an EU. That was a bold vision that evoked for some, images of the Holy Roman empire but in modern form, and for others, it was something comparable to a federated United States of Europe. Here, ironically, it is the old notion of the European nation-state that now stands in the way of further development towards the kind of union their leaders are planning for.

Those who have observed the remarkable success of the Association of Southeast Asian Nations (ASEAN) would be keen to see that experiment go well too. The 10 member states are less ambitious than those in the EU. They are also more hopeful for ASEAN because most of them are still in the process of nation-building and not yet locked into deep national jealousies and fears. At the same time, because Southeast Asian polities are still developing to become nation-states, they are more sensitive about their respective sovereign rights. It is widely recognised that for them to have come this far is already an astonishing achievement, but it is not clear that with each member having only recently come to appreciate the need to build a nation-state, they will be prepared to move towards anything like a regional grouping comparable to a federal state.

The second arrangement or development is where people like the Scots, the Catalans and other ethnic communities contemplate the further division of their respective nation-states. They remind us that there are indeed many such groups in various parts of Asia and Africa that would be ready to follow their example and break away from "nation-states" that they no longer believe in. This would be an easy route to take if and when they find that their central administrations have become weak and divided, and other powers have declared that they have become "failed states". Also, should the breakaway efforts in Europe succeed, they could become the model for other groups. In particular, that would appeal to smaller ethnic groups in the socially pluralistic and less culturally integrated nation-states in the rest of the world. All of them would become vulnerable, not least those in Southeast Asia.

This Southeast Asian region is unlikely to forget what happened when the British denied India its full inheritance of the departing imperial power of "British India", and allowed the establishment of the separate Muslim state of Pakistan. That decision created an early example of "ethnic cleansing" and led to unceasing hostility along India's western borders. That was followed by the break-up of Pakistan into two and the creation of the state of Bangladesh. Closer to Singapore, the threat of secession in Aceh in Indonesia and the continual unrest in West Irian remind us that this region is not safe from border and regime changes.

Fortunately, the different national leaders around are still committed to the sacred task of building secure nation-states for their very complex mix of ethnic identities. It is unlikely that any of them will find secession of any kind acceptable but they will always have to ensure that there is enough wealth and power to manage the nation-state and keep the ideal afloat.

The third alternative arrangement to a world of nation-states for a Singapore that sees its future more as a global city than as a nation-state would be to look to the Hanseatic League example. It would, however, call for a great leap of the imagination to contemplate a future for a league of global city-states in today's world.

The Hanseatic League provided an effective zone of security over several centuries and was invaluable at a time when Europe did not have any structure of dependable order. There was nominally a single Holy Roman empire, but there was no authority that wielded enough power to enforce law and order over large swathes of territory. The League emerged to save the trading world of the Baltic and Northern Europe from piracy and anarchy, and was essential for mercantile survival under those conditions.

For cities and states like Singapore to contemplate anything like such an arrangement, there would have to be the expectation that the current international order might no longer be able to deal successfully with the protectionist impulses that threaten the global market economy. Such a league of cities could offer another layer of global governance. This could be developed within the current international order as long as the major powers agree to allow another channel for economic interdependence while political differences are being thrashed out among less friendly protagonists in another framework. Such city-state groupings need not replace the system of nation-states, but it could be an organisational unit that enhances the sense of global economic security when political and cultural conflicts prevail.

SOME SCENARIOS OF THE FUTURE GLOBAL ORDER AND HOME TRUTHS

Given the historical background and the possible alternatives to the nation-state, what I can offer are not answers to the question that has been posed but instead two scenarios of the global order and the future of nation-states, with comments on what seems likely and what seems not to be.

The first is: What if parts of the world decide not to deal with nation-states any further. Nation-states do not have to disappear but, should that happen, that would call for a world-state with the requisite power to control all states. That is most unlikely to succeed.

Assuming that nation-states survive but become dysfunctional or subservient to larger groupings, it is conceivable that two or more "imperial" states become powerful enough to divide the world. Each of them would organise bundles of subordinate partners (some, perhaps, called "allies") that do not insist on having sovereign "national" borders.

Under such conditions, it is possible for several regional (federal or confederal) groups of "states" to be organised. Each of them would then be united by common security, economic and cultural interests.

In this scenario, there is nothing to prevent organisations based on allied cities (or city-states, all pluralist and non-national) from being formed. They could, together, construct strong networks, but always with the consent of the large "empires" and/or federated or confederated groups that agree that such network-leagues could also be useful in serving everybody else's interests.

The second scenario is a differently mixed system, with some nation-states holding on to their sovereignty. Such a global mix could consist of all or some of the following:

- Big states that seek to ensure they remain secure nation-states.
- Big states that are expansionist, building their own "imperial" networks.
- Small states that survive by being closely tied to larger economic or cultural "empires", retaining their sovereignty only in name.
- Small states that seek safety by forming (regional) federated or confederated units.
- City-states that offer to serve all the others equally.

Both scenarios would produce systems that cannot guarantee stability. There will always be some states ("imperial" or "federated") that will seek to change or improve upon the status quo to promote their own interests.

In summary, I am not sure we can say that the nation-state was ever the key organisational unit of the international community. It is an historic ideal and has served as a useful political and economic unit because powerful countries that are empires in everything but name had agreed to a set of rules by which smaller countries have been able to function. These powers will, from time to time, set out the key principles of interstate organisational behaviour, and these principles will prevail until the next re-configuration of powers is constituted.

During each period of broad agreement, big, medium and small countries will work out acceptable layers of relationships in order to attain relative peace all round. What is likely to remain is an international community grouped and re-grouped around a few big powers. Smaller states may have to be content to serve as the allies, partners, vassals or satellites of protective big powers. Some will do their utmost to avoid that fate and try not to become weaker, either by forming regional groupings of nation-states or by establishing networks of city-states. These groupings will find safety in numbers to achieve certain objectives, but each of them will still have to find their place in the framework of big power consent.

CHAPTER 2

What if Globalisation Fails?

KHONG CHO-OON

We need to begin by asking ourselves why we are posing this question now. Would we have considered this question seriously even a year ago?

I have to say, it would have been unlikely.

What we see today, however, is the rise of an increasingly strident form of nationalism and concerns over globalisation failing are, indeed, growing. We have to take this question with the utmost seriousness, as it is a question that is especially germane in a discussion about the health of not just Singapore but the global order today.

GLOBALISATION AND ITS DISCONTENTS — SHELL SCENARIOS

The great era of globalisation that now appears to be drawing to a close, began with the post-war recovery of Europe and Japan from the mid-20th century onwards. At that time, we witnessed the emergence of the so-called "Asian Tigers", East Asian countries that went through rapid economic development after the Second World War. These included Singapore, from the 1970s, followed by the opening-up of China with Deng Xiaoping's reforms from 1978. Margaret Thatcher in the United Kingdom and Ronald Reagan of the United States spearheaded radical market liberalisation in the 1980s, and we then saw the collapse of Soviet communism from 1989 to 1991.

It seemed to many that a brave new world of progress, peace and harmony was dawning. Globalisation was like an inexorable force. Through the spread of new technology and market liberalisation, it was a fundamental cornerstone belief that shaped our understanding of the global environment in which we live. Francis Fukuyama wrote his famous *End of History* thesis.

In the 1990s and in Shell's scenarios of the future, we talked about "TINA" by which we meant that "There Is No Alternative" to globalisation, market liberalisation and the advance of technology.[1] At the same time however, we recognised that globalisation carried within it the seeds of its own possible destruction.

In 1995, the company's scenario-planning team came up with two scenarios — one, titled "Just Do It" which celebrated the continued advance of globalisation and the spread of global markets; the other, presciently, we gave it a Chinese name *Da Wo* or "Big Me", and argued that globalisation would come up against governments which would act in a way that would restrain globalisation. They would have interests they would want to protect, societies would seek to preserve their cohesion, and the politics of identity would act to filter and hold back the forces of globalisation.

In 2001, the Shell scenarios team came up with another concept, that of "Heartland versus Edges", a division between, on the one hand, traditional values rooted in culture and history, and on the other hand, an outward orientation and global identity that is disconnected from its heartland roots. This division, we noted, ran through countries, societies and even individuals. This understanding gave us two new scenarios — one titled "Prism", a story of the heartlands resisting globalisation, motivated by forces that do not have their roots in economic soil, and "Business Class", which spoke of the rise of a cosmopolitan global elite, setting the terms on which the world would run. These scenarios led, of course, in markedly different directions.

This period of globalisation, I believe, came to an end, signalled by the Western financial crisis of 2008.

It was in that same year, 2008, that Shell also highlighted the critical challenge that climate change poses for us. In our global scenarios of 2008,

---

[1] The scenarios are based on plausible assumptions and quantification, and they are designed to stretch management thinking and even to consider events that may only be remotely possible. Scenarios therefore, are not intended to be predictions of likely future events or outcomes. Accordingly, investors should not rely on them when making an investment decision with regard to Royal Dutch Shell plc securities.

we made clear that we cannot continue using energy in the same way we have always done, and that a critical energy transition is inevitable.

Climate change had always been part of our scenarios, going back to the 1990s, but from 2008 onwards, climate and the implications for energy, took front and centre stage of our long-term global scenarios.

In our current global scenarios developed in 2013, "Mountains and Oceans", we repeated the challenge that we face from climate change; but we emphasised that at the same time that the world faces a critical global energy transition, we would also confront a range of other critical transitions in the global economy, in geopolitics and in governance.

Recovery from the 2008 financial crisis has proven to be difficult. We sense that there is no way of going back to what economists once called "The Great Moderation".

One of those transitions is a shift of geopolitical and economic power from West to East. This has proven to be highly disruptive for some, but on the other hand, highly invigorating and empowering for those who have gained from it. At the same time, we see people, in all parts of the world, demanding change from governing elites who have lost legitimacy and have grown too complacent with their sense of entitlement over their positions of power.

So what lies ahead?

A PERIOD OF SYNCHRONOUS CRITICAL TRANSITIONS TO POSSIBLE, NEW FORMS OF GLOBALISATION

We are indeed seeing a number of critical transition points come together — in economics, politics and energy, and they are doing so in an increasingly interconnected world. We are moving into an era of volatile transitions. As such, the nature of globalisation, as we have known it, will have to change too.

We may get a smooth transformation of the system, but it is unlikely as transitions, by their very nature, are inherently unstable. As Mao Tse-tung said, "A revolution is not a dinner party." We are moving into a more fluid geopolitical environment, with much greater political uncertainty and the danger of an increasingly confrontational world. The global order may well be heading into a period of disorder, before the system gels again to establish a new order. How much disorder there will be, or how much order we might get in this transitional period will depend on the choices that we as people and our governments make.

So will globalisation fail? Let me be clear. The technological component of globalisation which increases connectivity will not fail. Knowledge cannot be taken away. Yet, technology is just the carrier of globalisation. Globalisation will carry on but as John Gray, the eminent English political philosopher who has worked with us at Shell over many years, has argued, globalisation has no inherent tendency to promote either free markets or liberal democracy (Gray, 2005).

What could and will change is our understanding of, and hence our attitudes towards connectivity, with its promises and perils. This will in turn affect our practice of globalisation, how we use globalisation to shape the way we live, how we interact with others, as individuals, societies and states.

Globalisation is, therefore, changing, as the old model may be seen to be failing, but globalisation itself will not fail. Rather, it is up to us and the choices that we make, that will determine whether globalisation shapes a world for the better or for the worse.

Globalisation could move in one of two possible directions.

In one possible scenario — we call it "Mountains" — states take the lead. Mountains is a world of state power. It is capitalist, but it is not liberal.

Globalisation continues, but it slows, as it increasingly collides with a resurgent nationalism. People do not trust markets to provide what they need and will turn to governments to protect them from the destabilising impact of globalisation. Nationalism and national competition intensify over time.

Here's the rub: Countries will have to learn not to confront one another, but to get along with each other. They realise that it is only by working together that they will be able to tackle the challenges of climate change, resource scarcity and global demographics that confront the global community. Tackling those problems given their transboundary nature will require hard choices. After all, no one country, not even the most powerful, will be able to deal with these problems on its own. If we do not manage to find a way to work together, we will fail and the consequences will be profound. None of us will be able to isolate ourselves from these consequences.

In our other scenario which we call "Oceans", it is people power, rather than government, that re-shapes globalisation. A new, more vocal politics gathers momentum and pushes change. It is driven by an awakening and increasingly vigorous civil society that challenges government and seeks solutions outside of the public sphere. The debate on climate change takes place between generations; the debate on education takes place between parents and non-parents; ruling elites are challenged by new information technology-empowered "netizen" communities. This is a more decentralised, diffused form of globalisation.

Over the next decade, as different countries and societies engage with globalisation, each will put its own distinctive cultural, social, economic and political stamp onto it. Instead of TINA, we will have "TARA", "There Are Real Alternatives". Globalisation in its new form provides a menu of alternative choices.

To conclude, globalisation is transmuting into new forms, very different from today, and posing a different set of opportunities and costs for us. How we negotiate these new challenges will ultimately determine the form that globalisation takes, and our eventual fate.

REFERENCES

Gray, J. (2005, August 11). The world is round. *The New York Review of Books*. Retrieved from: www.nybooks.com/articles/2005/08/11/the-world-is-round/.

CHAPTER 3

What if Singapore Has to Choose Between China and the United States?

JOSEPH LIOW

THE PRESENT GEOSTRATEGIC CONTEXT

With regard to what the present global and regional uncertainties portend for Singapore, the task of predicting the future is made more challenging by the difficulties involved in divining what the regional strategy of the United States (US) will look like under the presidency of Donald Trump.

Currently, America's Asia policy remains long on statements and short on substance. This may not be all that bad given the impression conveyed during the course of the Trump election campaign that the new president was intent on overturning the table on the prevailing global order and, closer to home, adopting an adversarial approach towards China. However, these are early days yet, and even though I have my doubts, it remains to be seen if President Trump would indeed translate his antagonistic views on China into actual policies.

Of course, the point can be made that the Trump administration's withdrawal from the trade pact across 12 countries, the Trans-Pacific Partnership (TPP), is a worrying portent. Indeed, this move — via President Trump's first presidential executive order no less — has thrown into serious doubt American interest in and commitment to the trade and economic agenda of the fastest-growing region in the world.

Yet we might wish to keep what has happened with the TPP in perspective and do that on at least three counts. First, the TPP is not quite dead yet.

Technically, to salvage the TPP, all that the remaining 11 signatories have to do is to commit to amending the enactment rules so that US participation is no longer required for the implementation of the deal. Of course, the absence of the US would dilute the significance, if not the value, of the agreement, but that is a different prospect to not having a TPP at all.

Second, the fate of American commitment to the TPP would have hung in the balance anyway under a new administration, regardless of who won the presidency. Lest we forget, almost all the presidential candidates on both sides of the divide, opposed the TPP. This included Hilary Clinton, the Democratic Party's candidate for the presidency, ironically an architect of the agreement. She may have been more amenable had she won, but she would not have reneged on a campaign promise. That would have meant that the TPP would have had to undergo fresh rounds of negotiation before the US was prepared to reconsider joining, let alone come on-board eventually.

Third, even if Trump has withdrawn the US by dint of a presidential executive order, there is every chance that a new administration further down the road might revive American interest in the TPP.

While 2016 was a watershed year for the US, 2017 will see significant political developments in China. This year will witness the leadership of the Chinese Communist Party (CCP) assemble for the 19th Party Congress. After a successful sixth Plenary Session of the CCP in October 2016 which saw the party rally around the "core leadership" of President Xi Jinping, it is widely expected that Xi will consolidate power by overseeing the appointment and retention of his key supporters and allies in the powerful Politburo Standing Committee. Although the prospects of any significant obstacle being placed before Xi appears remote at this point, consolidation may yet prove to be less straightforward than one might assume. For starters, given President Trump's penchant for off-the-cuff statements (and tweets), Xi will be cautious in his response to any Trumpian provocation on Sino-US relations. On one hand, Xi certainly cannot afford to appear weak in the face of any such provocation. Yet on the other hand, he would need to be careful not to over-stoke nationalist sentiments and hazard too strong a position in response lest such a move leads to an escalation that he is unable to walk away from without risking his own domestic credibility.

It is against this backdrop of uncertainty that the question arises: "What if Singapore has to choose between China and the US?" If you hope I will set out which of those powers Singapore should choose, then allow me to apologise from the very outset as I will disappoint you. This is because the matter of "choosing" is a deceptively simple way of approaching the complex problems that might confront us in the not-too-distant future.

The answer to such a question necessarily depends on a wide range of intervening variables and factors, such as what event or circumstances might prompt such a state of affairs, what sort of leadership resides in Washington, Beijing, or indeed, in Singapore at that particular point when a choice needs to be made, whether other regional states are confronted with the same dilemma, just to name a few. In other words, unless the scenario is fleshed out in sharper relief, it is difficult to answer this question in an informed manner. For that reason, perhaps what is more useful for us is to take a step back and look at this question in terms of its assumptions and implications. Before we consider the "what ifs", let us consider the "what was" or "what it used to be".

TAKING STOCK OF SOUTHEAST ASIA'S BALANCING ACT

It is fair to state, and there will be a consensus on this, that since the end of the Cold War, we have had a strategic equilibrium in East Asia that centred on stable Sino-US relations. That equilibrium allowed the region to flourish economically while at the same time kept the centrifugal forces of strategic competition very much at bay, or at least contained.

There are, now, concerns that things are in danger of unravelling and that we are on the cusp of change, not least with the inauguration of the Trump administration in the US. This is a deep anxiety that American interest and engagement in Southeast Asia are going to recede.

At the same time, China continues to be assertive in its foreign relations in the region and this will gather pace. There will obviously be positive elements in the form of its economic outreach especially through trade and investments into the region, but there is also another dimension to it which we have seen in recent times — what I would call political or diplomatic browbeating. China appears to have a fairly straightforward approach on this score: China is a great power and it expects deference from its neighbours for which it is prepared to reward them handsomely. Conversely, it need not countenance the recalcitrance of smaller states who refuse to accept this "fact" and all that it implies.

As for Singapore, our leaders have always stressed that the country works hard to ensure that we are not placed in a position where we have to choose between the two great powers; or any other set of powers for that matter. In the context of Sino-US relations, our leaders have been especially careful not to take sides. This has become a constant refrain, and is illustrated implicitly in the following comments made by the late founding prime minister of Singapore, Lee Kuan Yew, with regard to Sino-US rivalry:

> If the United States attempts to humiliate China, keep it down, it will assure itself an enemy. If instead it accepts China as a big, powerful, rising state and gives it a seat in the boardroom, China will take that place for the foreseeable future. So if I were an American, I would speak well of China, acknowledge it as a great power, applaud its return to its position of respect and restoration of its glorious past, and propose specific, concrete ways to work together. Why should the United States take on China now when it knows that doing so will create an unnecessary adversary for a very long time, and one that will grow in strength and will treat it as an enemy? It is not necessary (cited in Allison and Blackwill, 2013).

Yet it is the very backdrop that we are confronted with today, with all the uncertainties mentioned above, that is compelling us to consider the question that was posed.

It does not help that, if one looks at the latest reporting on developments in Sino-Malaysian and Sino-Philippines relations, these have been cast precisely in this language of (Manila and Kuala Lumpur) choosing between the two powers. Which power are Malaysians and Filipinos portrayed as choosing to align with? According to many media reports, they have all but hopped onto the Chinese bandwagon. The assumptions underlying such accounts however, warrant closer scrutiny. Although it is undeniable that Manila and Kuala Lumpur have deepened bilateral relations with Beijing in recent months, there is no reason why this, on its own, should occasion any suspicion or cause trepidation that the Philippines and Malaysia have gravitated into a Chinese sphere of influence. All countries, including the US, Japan, and even Taiwan, have endeavoured to improve relations with China in recent years. Given the size of the Chinese economy and potential of its consumer market, it would be foolish for any country not to pursue relations with China. At the same time, it would be equally foolhardy to conclude that improving relations with China *ipso facto* means distancing oneself from the US. President Rodrigo Duterte's extensively-covered anti-imperialist rhetorical broadsides notwithstanding, there is little concrete evidence so far that the Philippines is turning its strategic gaze away from the US in any practical sense. Despite President Duterte's threats to end the Philippine alliance with the US, bilateral military exercises between the Philippine and American armed forces continued in 2016, and will do so in 2017 although there are suggestions that these would be reviewed in 2018 (Magan, 2016; Houck, 2016; *The Straits Times*, 2016). Nor are there any indications that Malaysia has in any way downgraded or de-prioritised the US in its foreign policy agenda. At the very least, it is still too early to tell whether decades of *Pax Americana* that have prevailed in the region — especially with regard to security ties between the US and these Southeast Asian countries — is giving way to a *Pax Sinica* for regional states with hitherto close defence ties with the US. On this score, we should bear in mind that although it requires conscious and deliberate effort, the historical record attests to Southeast Asia's ability to balance and engage a range of external powers with different degrees of success, whilst still preserving some measure of autonomy.

THE LIKELIHOOD OF OPEN CONFLICT BETWEEN THE US AND CHINA

Before we consider the scenarios and conditions governing this issue of choice, let us take yet another step back. This notion of choosing sides conjures images of a zero-sum game; one that involves trade-offs; where choosing one side suggests that you are automatically distancing yourself from the other. We have, in a sense, seen this before. During the Cold War, the intense rivalry between the US and the Soviet Union which took place on a global scale, made it exceedingly difficult for smaller states to maintain neutrality or to remain non-aligned, the efforts of the Afro-Asian Movement and Non-Aligned Movement notwithstanding. We live in a different world today, and under present conditions where everything is increasingly interdependent, interconnected and digital technology-driven, talk of choosing sides between the US and China represents a false dichotomy, predicated on flawed assumptions. Let me set out my reasons for saying this especially with regard to US-China relations.

First, I believe that Chinese leaders will, in private, grudgingly admit that the US has had a restraining hand on Japan and Taiwan in this region. We have to bear in mind that relations with Japan as well as with Taiwan, are consequential foreign policy issues for the US as far as its policy towards Asia is concerned. It is quite possibly even more so for decision-makers in Beijing. For China, its rivalry with Japan is arguably more complex and acrimonious than its rivalry with the US. As for Taiwan, the Chinese leadership appears to be operating on the assumption that time is on their side when it comes to cross-Strait relations. I am not entirely sure if this is the right way to think about it. As the years pass, efforts to create and strengthen a sense of Taiwanese national identity will surely sink deeper roots, and if this happens, peaceful resolution of cross-Strait relations will be all the more difficult. Given the considerable challenges Beijing faces in dealing with Japan and Taiwan on their own terms, the American contribution to the stability of these sets of relationships by virtue of Washington's restraining influence on Tokyo and Taipei have been and will be instrumental in maintaining relative peace in the region. In other words, even if Beijing is interested to limit the strategic reach of the US in the region, that does not mean that it wants the US to be entirely disengaged from it.

Second, while the Trump presidency might scale back some of its interest and commitment in the region, it is not likely to disengage on its own accord from the region entirely as well. Yes, the halcyon days of the Obama administration's pivot to Asia are gone and will not return any time soon. But "Trumpism" notwithstanding, I think the US not only has much to offer to the region, the former also has much to gain from the latter in terms of economics and security. More importantly, I think that senior cabinet officials as well as Republican Party elders are aware of that, even if President Trump seems nonchalant about it. In point of fact, on the security front, US policy towards the region in the early months of the Trump administration has thrown up more continuity than change with Secretary of Defence James Mattis's assurances to Tokyo and Seoul, and President Trump's reinforcement of these assurances to Prime Minister Shinzo Abe on the occasion of their summit in February 2017.

The economic story, however, might admittedly hold out discomfiting prospects for change. President Trump is clearly intent on rectifying what he and the China hawks in his administration deem to be unfair trade practices on China's part, and they have consequently taken a hard line on China. Underscoring this view is a crucial but implicit assumption: the US has sufficient economic leverage to hurt China more than China can hurt US interests. This is a dangerously misguided assumption.

Let us consider some facts: China is currently the third largest market for US exports, letting in US$104 billion of goods in 2016. Even though this figure has fallen marginally over the last couple of years, with the size of the Chinese market, its increasing affluence and emerging middle class, China will still be a consequential destination for American goods and services. China is also a key node in the global supply chain on which much of US industry relies. While the Trump administration could, in theory, replace Chinese labour with American workers, it is all but certain that this would drive up labour costs for American companies, which in turn could have a negative effect on productivity that has already been on the decline. In other words, the cost of production for US industry will doubtless increase under conditions which President Trump seeks to create, and this cost will ultimately be transferred to the American consumer. Whether President Trump is aware of this or is prepared to admit it, Americans have become avid consumers of Chinese goods. The US is the largest market for Chinese products, which in turn accounts for the sizeable trade deficit between the two countries. While China would obviously be hurt by higher tariffs, raising them will also have a significant impact for consumption patterns of the average American.

In other words, the Trump administration might soon realise that the interests of the American people are better served by more conciliatory methods of rectifying the trade imbalance with China.

Third, following on from the previous point is the fact that China is already an economic powerhouse with growing political influence. This influence will only increase in the coming years with the One Belt One Road initiative and the Asian Infrastructure Investment Bank. So, omitting or eliminating Beijing from the regional equation is simply ludicrous. It is a difficult thing to imagine, and impossible to implement.

Fourth, we need to remember that, rhetoric aside, the scope and depth of bilateral relations between the US and China have widened and deepened considerably over the years. Not too long ago, bilateral relations essentially focused on a small basket of issues: cross-Strait relations, exchange rate of the *renminbi* and bilateral trade. Over the last few years, it has expanded to cover a wider range of issues. Here we are talking about territorial disputes, regional economic trade initiatives and other global issues like climate change, non-proliferation, counterterrorism and cybersecurity. The number of official and unofficial channels for them to discuss these issues have also increased. To that effect, it is notable that Secretary of State Rex Tillerson acknowledged the broad scope of Sino-US relations during his recent visit to Beijing.

So simply put, this bilateral relationship is the most complex relationship between two great powers that the world has ever seen. Their interests intertwine and overlap in ways that makes the prospect of open conflict between them difficult to fathom.

SO WHAT IF WE HAVE TO CHOOSE?

Let us nonetheless think about that scenario of Singapore having to choose sides. What sort of conditions would lead us to such a scenario? In other words, let me contradict all that I have argued earlier and draw out some possible scenarios. Let me discuss five.

First is the election of an unpredictable, impulsive, self-absorbed, vengeful president in the US who would refuse to heed the counsel of others. Needless to say, this is a concern with the current president. However, regardless of the validity of misgivings towards President Trump's character and personality, not to mention his lack of political experience, we have to bear in mind that he has in fact surrounded himself with a very strong national security and foreign policy team. James Mattis, H. R. McMaster and John Kelly are strong and respected leaders with accomplished military credentials. None of them are "yes men". While there are concerns that as secretary of state, Tillerson has yet to demonstrate leadership in what is seen as the most senior cabinet position, few doubt his credentials and professional qualities honed in the private sector. At the same time, there are undeniable reservations about Steve Bannon, Donald Trump's presidential advisor and chief ideologue, as well as the China hawks who populate the trade office and commerce department, including Robert Lighthizer, Wilbur Ross and Peter Navarro.

Second is that of nationalist hawks tightening their grip on power in China. They may be found predominantly but not solely in the People's Liberation Army, and this is the segment of Chinese society that has no reservations when it comes to thinking, talking and planning for conflict with the US. More importantly, they have no patience to suffer the anxieties of small states which may be caught in-between that conflict. They believe that the rise of China is inevitable and that the US and its friends are basically standing in its way.

Third is if there is a serious breakdown in Sino-US relations, which obviously is a scenario that flows from the first and second scenarios. In this case, we are envisaging a situation akin to the Cold War and all those images conjured by the Thucydides Trap, and discussions emerging from that. Even then, as I have written elsewhere, choosing sides under such circumstances is likely to be as costly a decision for a small state like Singapore as standing on the sidelines (Liow, 2017).

Fourth is if an implicit agreement emerges between the US and China to create spheres of influence or rather spheres of predominant interests as it is unlikely either is going to be willing to cede influence in a particular region completely to the other. The South China Sea would be an interesting bellwether of that possibility because it seems unlikely that the US under Trump, or even under Obama at the time, will be prepared to go out of its way to defend the Philippines' interests over a few features that are submerged at high tide.

Fifth is the scenario of a failure of Singapore's diplomacy. For a good part of the post-Vietnam War era, Singapore has worked hard to avoid being put in the sort of situation that is being contemplated here. This being the case, if our leaders find themselves in a position where they have no choice but to choose sides between the two superpowers, it essentially implies that the diplomatic and political elite of the day may well have failed to "hold the line."

CHOOSING SIDES: THE TERMS

Finally, if we did find ourselves in that position of having to choose between alignment with the US or China, the follow-up question would be: On what terms would we make that choice? Let me offer some thoughts on this.

First, if we choose, we must choose on the basis of interests, not countries. It may be a cliché, but it is worth reiterating that we are pro-interests not pro-this or pro-that power. Also, any choice that is made cannot be made at gunpoint (whether literally or figuratively). It has to be an informed choice to secure Singapore's national interests, and it is a choice that would have to be conveyed to the people; their support and endorsement will have to be secured.

Second, if we choose, it must be understood that there should be no interference in domestic politics by that power. In reality, this is likely to be difficult because if we were to capitulate and make concessions, it would be a slippery slope where we would be expected to make even more concessions over time. Keeping that influence and those expectations at bay will be a challenge for the government of the day in Singapore.

Third, we have to be mindful of the perceptions created in our neighbourhood. If making a choice means making concessions, we must be very careful of the signals that are being sent in the process of doing that. Simply put, we may send the wrong signals or other states may read the wrong signals and draw the wrong conclusions from our actions — that Singapore is a pushover. It would not be in our interest to send such a signal, consciously or otherwise. Bear in mind that Singapore is not unfamiliar with bullies.

Fourth, we need to remember that the US and China are not the only major powers of consequence in the region. Again, the question has been cast in that way, but the reality is likely to be considerably more complex. The Sino-US relationship is going to be a key feature of regional affairs in the foreseeable future, but it is not going to be the only determinant of the regional geopolitical landscape. Other powers will also matter, such as Japan, India, Australia and even Russia. Singapore will have to continue deepening our relationships with them too even as we keep one eye constantly trained on developments in Sino-US relations.

Finally, there is ASEAN. It is probably not the best time to talk about ASEAN unity. Indeed, ASEAN has seen better days as far as its unity and cohesion are concerned. Nevertheless, we need to be mindful of the fact that small states in Southeast Asia are facing the same challenge, the same dilemma with regard to the US and China. It is not something that Singapore alone will be confronted with. Other states in the region are pondering how to navigate the waters of great power politics. I think it would be very useful for Singapore to not just look at the situation from purely the point of view of what Singapore's interests are, but also in relation to, and in cohesion with our neighbours who are facing similar challenges. However weak ASEAN may be, there is still strength in numbers, and this strength will afford us some much-needed autonomy from the centrifugal forces of great power politics, provided ASEAN can indeed remain united.

REFERENCES

Allison, G., & Blackwill, R. (2013, March 5). Interview: Lee Kuan Yew on the future of US-China relations. *The Atlantic*. Retrieved from: https://www.theatlantic.com/china/archive/2013/03/interview-lee-kuan-yew-on-the-future-of-us-china-relations/273657/.

Houck, C. (2016, November 15). US troops are still in the Philippines, despite Duterte's insults and threats. *Defence One*. Retrieved from: http://www.defenseone.com/news/2016/11/us-troops-are-still-philippinesregardless-what-duterte-says/133195/.

Magan, G. (2016, October 4). Philippines, US joint military exercises despite Duterte's comments. *Philippine News*. Retrieved from: https://philnews.ph/2016/10/04/Philippines-us-hold-joint-military-exercises-despite-dutertes-comments/.

Liow, J. C. (2017, January 22). Trump's ascent should prompt Southeast Asia to look back. *Nikkei Asian Review*. Retrieved from: https://asia.nikkei.com/Viewpoints/Joseph-Chinyong-Liow/Trump-s-ascent-should-prompt-Southeast-Asia-to-look-back.

The Straits Times. (2016, September 29). Philippines says joint military exercise with US to go ahead in 2017, but will review 2018 drills. Retrieved from: http://www.straitstimes.com/asia/se-asia/philippines-say-will-go-ahead-with-joint-military-exercise-with-us-in-2017-but.

SECTION **II**

Looking In

CHAPTER 4

What if Non-Economic Indicators Become the Measure of a Country's Progress?

JEREMY AU

THE INADEQUACIES OF GDP AS A MEASURE OF A COUNTRY'S PROGRESS

For many years now, I have had a fascination with the question: What is progress? What is growth and progress to the individual, the family, and the community? Here is what I have learnt.

When we are with our children, we know what growth is. Growth is the change in their levels of self-awareness and ability between yesterday and today. We also know that our children are defined by much more than their capacity to produce wealth or to consume it, although I must say they seem to do a lot of both.

Yet, when we talk about Singapore as a nation which encompasses millions of individual human beings, we somehow invert the model. We use gross domestic product (GDP) and other economic metrics to measure our progress as a society and country. As you know, growth in Singapore is commonly described this way:

One percent: "Ah!"
Negative one percent: "Not so good."
Five percent: "Excellent!"
Negative five percent: "Terrible!"

So why is it that what should be self-evident about human growth and progress is somehow not put into practice for a community of 5 million human individuals in Singapore? The answer is that GDP is easy, simple and clear. It is good for what it is designed to do — to measure production at a national level. It is an objective metric that all of us can agree on — the value of what is produced in this country.

You can use this metric to measure performance at different points of time, such as the value of what was produced in year 2006, 2010, or 2016. It is simple to communicate: $290 billion of production last year is good; and $300 billion of national production this year is even better. That is also why it becomes so easy to use it as a benchmark for decision-making at a policy level and at a community level. It makes it so easy to speak about and to show improvement or progress to anyone.

However, GDP was never designed to measure societal progress. To some extent, we know that our gross national product is correlated with individual wealth, which is in turn correlated with life satisfaction. We also know that Singapore is one of the world's most prosperous countries on a per capita basis, that is, if we take the GDP of the country and divide that by the number of Singapore residents there are, assuming each has an equal share. Yet any Singaporean can also tell you that this does not mean we feel happy, or prosperous, or that we feel that there has been progress. Economic measures simply fail to capture the totality of what Singapore's progress means as a country, and whether people perceive that progress has taken place at all.

HUNT FOR A BETTER MEASURE

So, where does that leave us? If we can measure the entirety of Singapore's progress, we can then improve on that, and we already intuitively understand this as a society. We see this with our focus on global rankings for quality of life, labour markets and economic conditions. Yet these rankings are still inadequate because they only measure isolated facets of Singapore's progress and are always used in comparison with other countries.

That is why across the world, leaders have always sought improved measurements of progress at the national level. The range of measures that have been used includes the United Nations Development Programme's Human Development Index which measures life expectancy, literacy and standard of living, taking into account the gender diversity of these experiences. It also includes the Social Progress Index developed by the Social Progress Initiative that covers an even wider range of measures to do with access to the basics in life, sense of well-being and respect for rights and choice.

Three years ago, then IPS S R Nathan Fellow Mr Ho Kwon Ping delivered five lectures on the future of Singapore. I was there at his last lecture when he called for the development of a uniquely Singaporean human development index which would measure our overall well-being. He noted that it would have to be holistic, measurable and aspirational for all Singaporeans.

I actually stood up at that time, and I asked him a question: "What would go into this index?" He very politely laughed and answered that he would leave it to others to define the index. It has been three years since and here is my answer.

Where would we find a set of holistic values that all Singaporeans aspire to? What can we base an index and form of measurement upon? Despite all the discussion of what it would encompass, the answer is actually pretty simple. Hint: We recited it every day as kids. It is the National Pledge.

> We, the citizens of Singapore, pledge ourselves as one united people, regardless of race, language or religion, to build a democratic society based on justice and equality, so as to achieve happiness, prosperity and progress for our nation.

Simple words, powerful language.

Yet, we leave it behind after our days as schoolchildren. Where do we use it today other than at our national events? This is what we can base the alternative index of progress on — the core values that we aspire towards as found in the Pledge — unity, racial harmony, democracy, justice, equality, happiness, prosperity and progress.

THE SINGAPORE DEVELOPMENT INDEX

So where would we find the metrics that are related to these values? How can we measure these values? What does it mean for people in Singapore? Thankfully, we have the Gallup World Poll. It polls people across 160 countries every year on 100 issues.

In Singapore, Gallup has conducted 1,100 face-to-face interviews annually since 2007 which leaves a margin of error of 3.8 percent to the data. The questions that they ask include, "What do Singaporeans think about Singapore?" This is what we can base our index on.

Values	Metrics	2016 Scores
Unity	Support from Society	92%
	Mutual Respect in Society	93%
Racial Harmony	Quality of Life for Minorities	87%
Democracy	Confidence in Honest Elections	90%
	Integrity of Government	97%
Justice	Confidence in Police	95%
	Confidence in Judiciary	89%
	Integrity of Business	96%
Equality	Meritocracy	84%
	Freedom for Life Choices	86%
Happiness	Satisfaction with Current Life	60%
	Feelings of Enjoyment	82%
Prosperity	Satisfaction with Standard of Living	88%
	Employment Opportunities	34%
Progress	Optimism for Life (5yrs)	69%
	Optimism for Living Standards (1yr)	45%
Singapore Development Index		80%

Table generated by Quad.sg based on Gallup World Poll (Gallup Organization, 2016).

So, it is time to review the data. In Singapore in 2016, for Unity, 92 percent of the respondents felt that they could get support from others in society in times of need; 93 percent felt respected in recent times by others in society. On Racial Harmony, 87 percent believed that there is a high quality of life for minorities in Singapore. With regard to Democracy, 90 percent said they were confident that elections in Singapore were clean, 97 percent believed that the government is free from corruption. As for Justice, 95 percent of the respondents said they had confidence in the police and 89 percent had confidence in the judicial system; 96 percent believed that business is free from corruption. As for Equality, 84 percent of the respondents believed that if one worked hard, one could get ahead. Also, 86 percent believed they were free to choose what they wanted to do with their lives. On Happiness, 60 percent of the respondents said they were satisfied with their lives at the time and about where they could be, and 82 percent said that they had felt positive feelings of joy and happiness in their lives in the recent past. On Prosperity, 88 percent said they were satisfied with their financial status and the standard of living in terms of what they could do and buy. However, only 34 percent of Singaporeans believed at the time of the survey that it was a good time for anyone to seek a job. On Progress, 69 percent were optimistic about their life in five years' time but only 45 percent of the respondents believed that their financial and living standards would improve in the next year.

This means that Singapore scores an average of 80 percent on the Singapore development index. I personally like to think of it as a PSLE score of 240, which means it is a credible mark.

SINGAPORE'S PROGRESS OVER TIME

What do these findings mean across time? It means that the Singapore Development Index has hovered from 70 percent to 80 percent despite the changes in the numbers of the annual year-on-year GDP economic growth. Yet there is a much more interesting story about how Singaporeans perceive our progress as a society relative to the values that we aspire to.

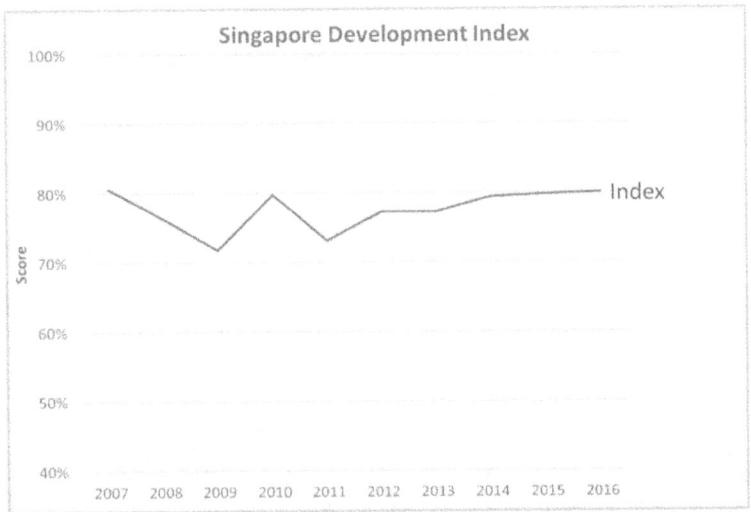

Chart generated by Quad.sg based on Gallup World Poll (Gallup Organization, 2016).

For Unity as a people, the score has improved from 81 percent to 92 percent, with a strong dip in 2010 to 2011.

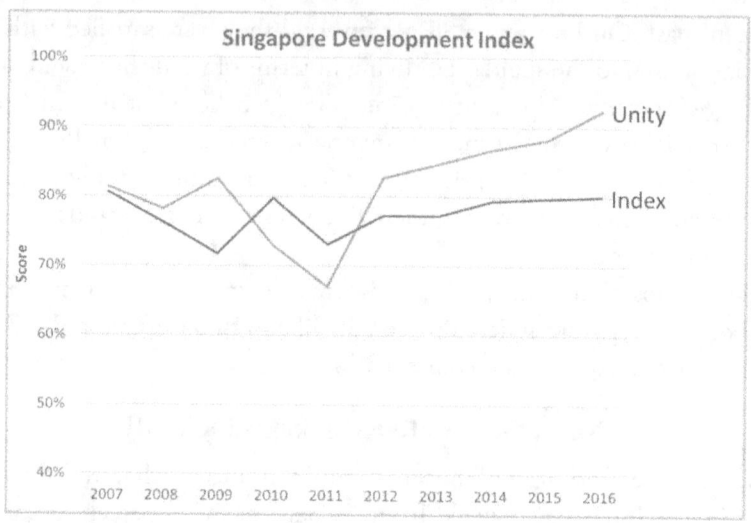

Chart generated by Quad.sg based on Gallup World Poll (Gallup Organization, 2016).

For Harmony, the score has stayed relatively high at 85 percent on average with a dip in 2011.

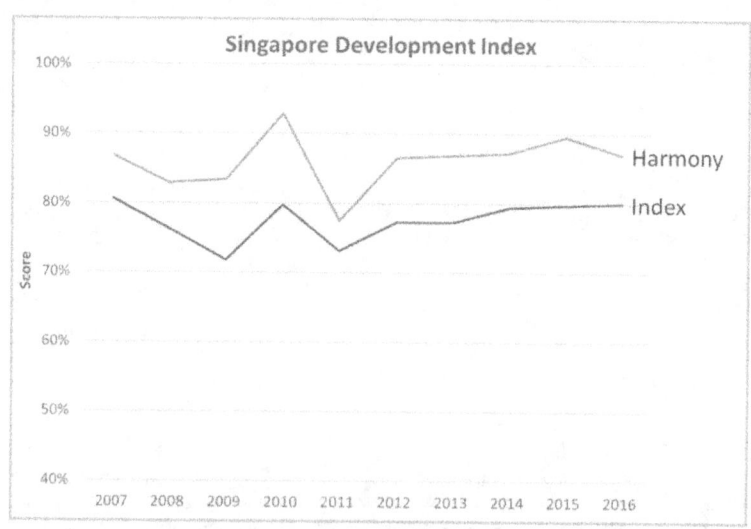

Chart generated by Quad.sg based on Gallup World Poll (Gallup Organization, 2016).

As for belief that Singapore is a strong democratic nation, the level of assent to that weakened in 2011 and 2012, and then recovered.

Non-Economic Indicators as Measure of Country's Progress

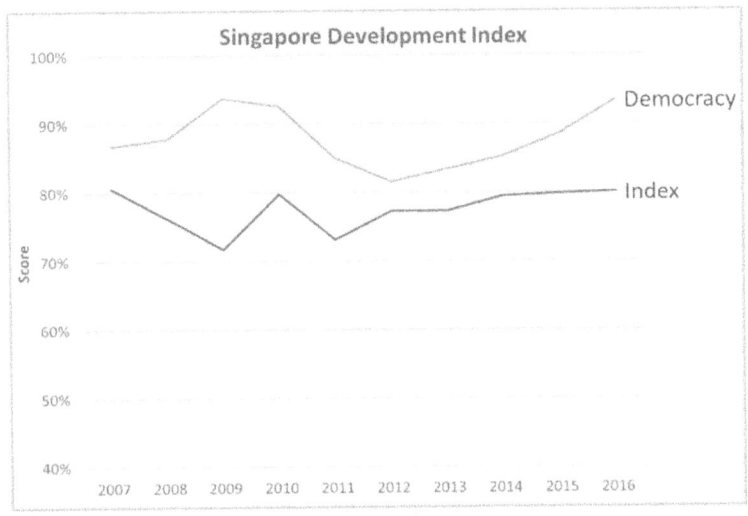

Chart generated by Quad.sg based on Gallup World Poll (Gallup Organization, 2016).

For Justice, there was a similar weakening in 2011 and 2012, with a recovery since then.

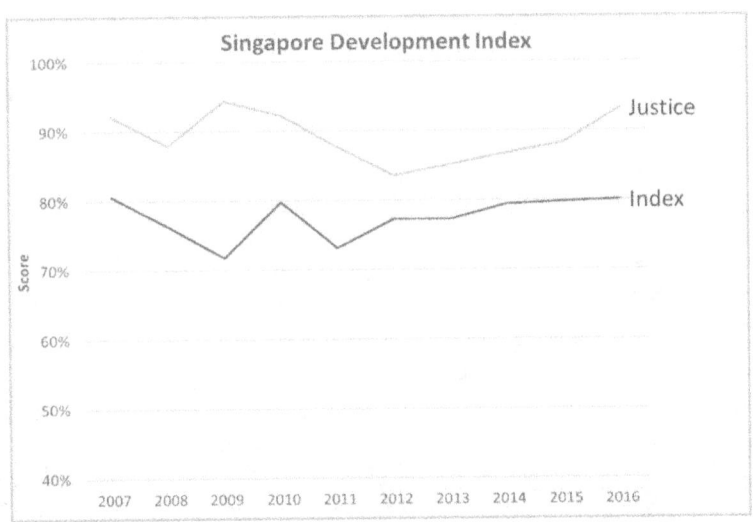

Chart generated by Quad.sg based on Gallup World Poll (Gallup Organization, 2016).

As for perceptions about the equality of opportunity and access to life options, there was a slight dip in 2008 with it mostly being flat across the recent 10 years.

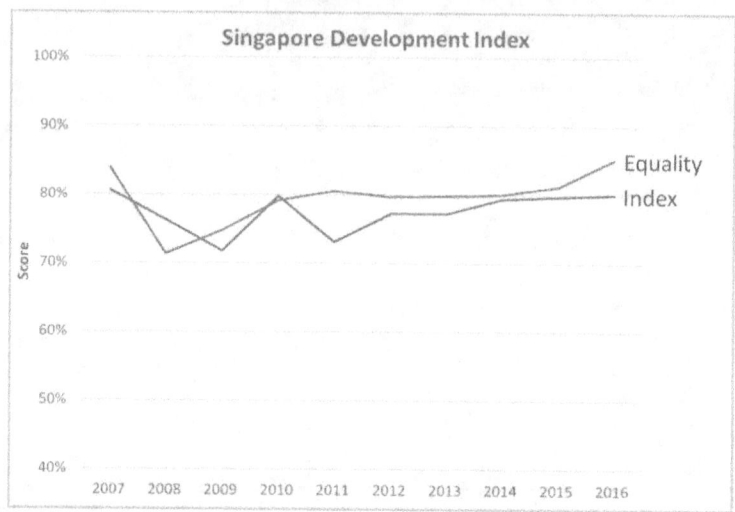

Chart generated by Quad.sg based on Gallup World Poll (Gallup Organization, 2016).

Happiness itself took a strong dip in 2009 and 2011, and has stayed at roughly 71 percent.

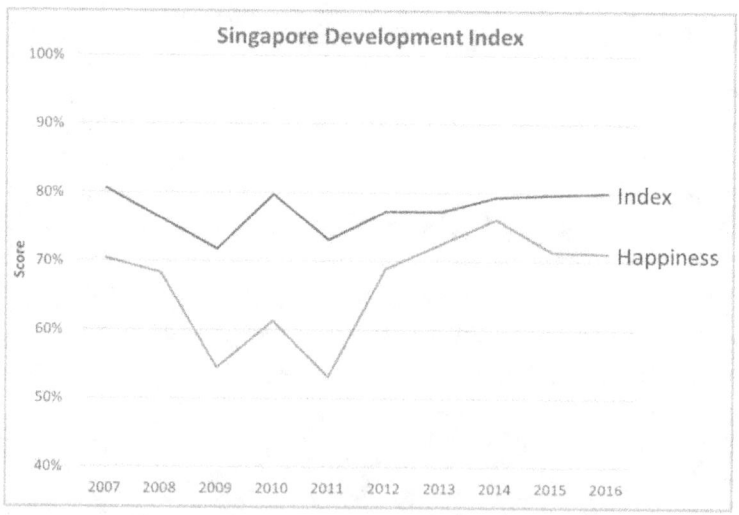

Chart generated by Quad.sg based on Gallup World Poll (Gallup Organization, 2016).

What is also interesting is that the perceptions of how prosperous Singapore is as a country took a sharp dip in 2009, recovered strongly in 2010, and has then gradually slid by 3 percentage points every year till today.

Non-Economic Indicators as Measure of Country's Progress

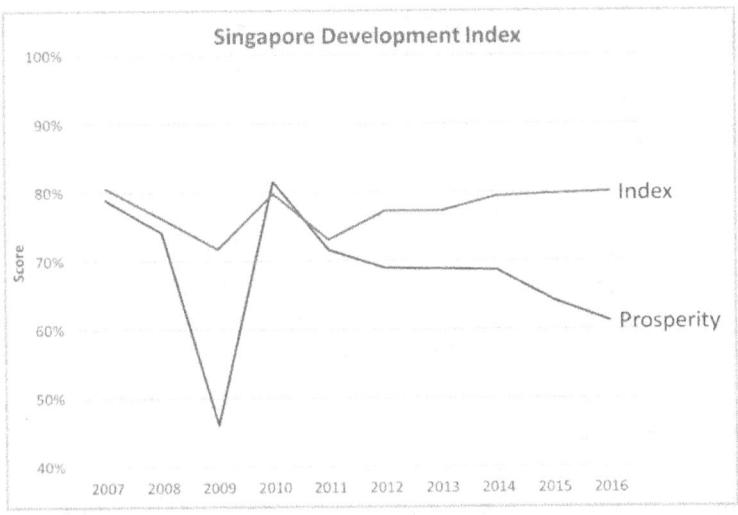

Chart generated by Quad.sg based on Gallup World Poll (Gallup Organization, 2016).

So people do not think Singapore is as prosperous as it used to be despite the GDP numbers and the like.

Next, there is optimism about Singaporeans' future standard of living and life. We can see that it has a cyclical nature with dips in 2009, 2012 and 2016. What we can tell is that the data shows some interactions with key events

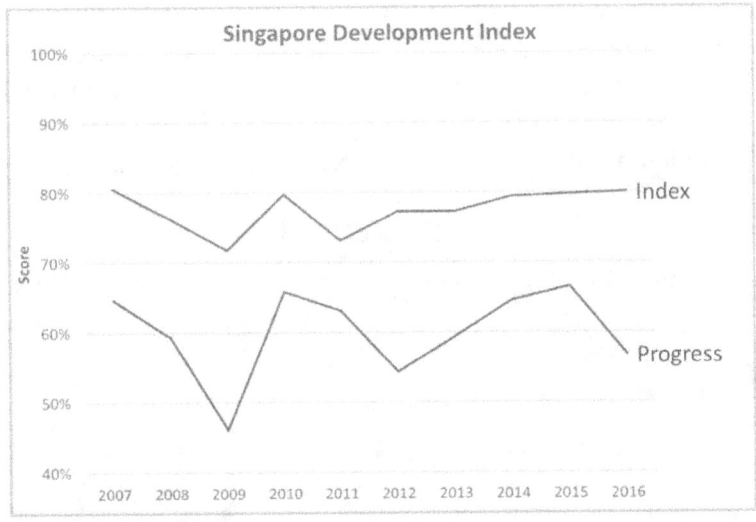

Chart generated by Quad.sg based on Gallup World Poll (Gallup Organization, 2016).

both external and internal. The 2008 financial crisis which was felt between 2009 and 2011 and the 2011 general election as well as the 2015 general election all seem to be interesting points that could account for changes in the national mood.

Looking at how Singaporeans perceive our country's progress relative to those values, we then understand that Singapore's social fabric as a whole has strengthened over the years. However, the belief, perception and the optimism regarding Singapore's economic vitality has dropped over time.

THE FUTURE

What does that mean for us? The Singapore Development Index can thus form the framework for future discussions on all sorts of issues in Singapore. For government policy proposals, we can use it to score and communicate the likely impact of these programmes and policies on our core values. It can be the new benchmark for discussion, measurement and tracking.

Last but not least, this set of measured values is not just a common language to rally academics and policymakers. It is a way to involve community stakeholders, social sector leaders and our business leaders so that they can help ensure that every facet of what it means for Singapore to progress is attended to.

In conclusion, with our children, we know that they are not perfect. Through their imperfections, we see how much they have truly grown as well as how to unlock their potential. With Singapore too, we know that our country is not perfect. Yet, by bravely recognising our imperfections, not only can we see how much we have actually grown as a nation over the years, but also how to unleash the extraordinary potential that is within.

REFRERENCES

Gallup Organization. (2016). Gallup World Poll 2016. New York: Gallup Press.

CHAPTER 5

What if Singapore Fails to Become a Creative and Innovative Nation?

AARON MANIAM

Metaphors matter.

Often seen as the exclusive tools of poets and other writers, they are critical in all our daily lives. Seemingly literal sentences like "Children blossom into adults" actually employ the metaphor of plants growing. When we set out to "defeat an argument", we are using military metaphors and treating discussion as a battle.

The original Greek word for metaphor (μεταφορά) refers to transportation — what started out as a description for transportation of physical things was, over time, applied to the transportation of meaning, where the qualities of one thing were used to describe another. George Lakoff and Mark Johnson rightly note that metaphors are among the things we "live by", shaping how we view issues and what we prioritise, or fail to (Lakoff & Johnson, 1980).

This essay uses a metaphor-based approach to examine three questions around Singapore's future as a creative, innovative nation:

- Why might we fail to be creative and innovative?
- Why does it matter if we fail?
- How might we avoid such failure?

WHY MIGHT WE FAIL TO BE CREATIVE AND INNOVATIVE?

This might arise because our metaphors for creativity and innovation are currently incomplete, at best, or mistaken, at worst.

Some of Singapore's most dominant metaphors cluster around engineering. When we speak of "structures" for creativity, or having education and economic "systems" that are conducive for innovation, we are utilising images of engineering, where input is subjected to processes in a system and generate some form of output. The language of engineering is often the language of machinery — cogs, gears and other components interact within a system to produce outcomes. According to such thinking, creative output can be produced once the right input and intervening processes are in place.

The other family of metaphors frequently deployed when discussing creativity and innovation is the market economy. In education, much debate has centred on whether students have the right "incentives" to be creative — grades, co-curricular points and the like. Our economic agencies often offer incentives to firms of all types and sizes if they can demonstrate the innovative potential of their ideas. These approaches reflect the fundamental view that creativity and innovation are driven by what is often described as "market forces": impartial analysis of costs and benefits, carried out by rational, utility-maximising agents.

There is nothing intrinsically wrong with engineering and market-based metaphors. Indeed, one might argue that it was precisely an unsentimental focus on both that catalysed some of Singapore's early and most lauded successes, like the creation of an industrial centre in and around Jurong. This policy measure was underpinned by the belief that the western part of Singapore could form a commercial nucleus around which companies gathered, and which relied on multinational corporations and local firms alike responding to market incentives.

However, an exclusive focus on engineering and the market can involve critical pitfalls. Such limitations apply to all metaphors — as much as they illuminate certain aspects in a thing, idea or issue, they can also lead us to under-emphasise or even overlook other important dimensions. In the case of engineering, its assumptions of linearity and predictability in systems fail to recognise the inherently surprising quality of creativity and innovation. It is no coincidence that many of the most creative practitioners in any field ascribe their work to "inspiration", a Muse or something similarly vague, volatile and intuitive. At heart, the creative process can be tamed but not totally structured; space needs to be set aside for its innate non-linearity and, some might say, whimsical nature.

Similarly, market assumptions about the primacy of incentives and cost-benefit analysis in determining human behaviour are inadequate when describing creativity and innovation. Some of this has to do with the fact that creativity cannot be "made to order", so incentives are at best, necessary, but insufficient to generate creative products. One could go further: creative and innovative outcomes possess worth that cannot be reduced to the quantifiable metrics of a market system. This is why so many works of art, and other creative output, are often described as "priceless", and why it goes against our aesthetic sensibilities and even moral instincts to try and "put a number" on how valuable a creative masterpiece might be.

WHY FAILURE MATTERS — TWO SCENARIOS

Taken to their logical conclusions, both engineering and market metaphors could pose problems for Singapore's long-term prospects as a creative and innovative nation.

For instance, excessive focus on engineering might turn us into a "Scientific Sahara" — as fully-structured, systematic, ordered and predictable as any of the best engineering systems, but fundamentally arid and soulless. Such a place would probably effectively imitate the creative products of others and be an effective second-mover, but not generate any creative output of its own. It would generate solutions and products for problems that are already well-known, but deal less effectively with relatively unprecedented situations that require agile, adaptive responses. One could of course argue that even a desert is an ecosystem, teeming with evolving life if we know where to look for it, but the broad point remains that a purely engineered system would have little room in it for dynamic vitality.

Over-emphasis on incentives, costs and benefits could lead to a scenario of "Market Mediocrity", because producers of both economic and other goods fail to move beyond the lowest common denominator. This would be a place where art, innovation and other creative output would be subject to market signals and resource optimisation: so we could well end up with mass produced echoes and shells of creativity, which use scarce resources highly efficiently, but with little deep innovation that genuinely speaks to the core of the human condition. This would be a place to make a *living*, and possibly a successful one by material indicators, but not necessarily to craft a meaningful *life*.

HOW CAN WE AVOID SUCH FAILURE?

The natural question at this stage is how Singapore might avoid the extreme, but unfortunately also plausible, scenarios sketched out above. Since metaphors by definition both magnify and mask, the answer cannot be to look for an elusive *single* and overarching metaphor that meets our needs. Instead, we have to adopt a more nuanced and refined *mix* of metaphors, where different images account for different aspects of an issue or idea. This means preserving the engineering and market metaphors explored earlier, supplementing rather than supplanting them with others to add overall richness and range. This section outlines two metaphors that could prove to be useful complements especially as we think about creativity and innovation.

Biology and ecology

First, the downsides of a pure engineering metaphor can be attenuated by metaphors from biology and ecology. In other words, it would be helpful to perceive creativity and innovation as the results of living, breathing and constantly evolving systems, not just clinically engineered ones. This is important so as to do justice to the nuance, adaptability, non-linearity and emergence of the creative process. Bob Johansen, former President of the Institute of the Future based in the United States, underscores the importance of such an approach in what he calls "biomimicry" (Johansen, 2009). He notes that an appreciation of the biological underpinnings of many human systems is one of 10 skills that will prove critical for leaders in an increasingly volatile, uncertain, complex and ambiguous (VUCA) world.

Ecological metaphors convey additional subtleties. Creativity and innovation can sometimes be stereotyped as only involving showy, glamorous elements — poetry, performing arts, fashion and the like. However, the reality for any creative practitioner often involves much more mundane aspects — sweaty rehearsals, poring through lighting plans for a performance, even failed attempts at pottery or sculpture. Similarly, ecologies survive not only through their most beautiful or even obvious elements; they thrive in part because of the muck and mire at the bottom of the food chain.

The same might be said of a creative and innovative nation — it involves not just the glitz of media headlines and international awards, but the daily reality of innovating to build, for instance, environmentally-friendly urban developments, like Singapore's current efforts in Punggol, as well as planning how to ensure thriving economic ecologies in places like Changi Business Park, the Jurong Town Corporation's Launchpad in Ayer Rajah and other industrial estates.

Gifts

A second useful set of metaphors revolves around what French sociologist Marcel Mauss calls the "gift economy" which transcends the language of markets (Mauss, 1966). In a gift economy, things can have intangible worth, even without quantifiable value. Such gifts could come from nature, for which gratitude is expressed in tribal or even modern harvest rituals. They could also be social, as seen in the practice of gift exchange during major festivals, and where exact numerical equivalence between gifts is often not seen as strictly necessary. Creative talents are a third category of gifts: they are not something we can earn purely by hard, deterministic work, but are often undeserved — hence the idea of something being *given*. As many artists and creative practitioners would attest, artists do not always control their gifts, and are at best stewards, trustees or channels for their expression. Gifts suggest different approaches to creativity and innovation, compared to Singapore's usual metaphors: different approaches to what we value, and how value is determined; different social attitudes towards exchange incentives; and different attitudes to how much we can plan as opposed to leave ourselves open to surprise, opportunities and serendipity.

Of course, a gift-based approach does not need to be arbitrary and self-indulgent. Indeed, one could argue that discipline and intentional (but not blind adherence to) structure are important, particularly for gifts to be well-used. Scholar Lewis Hyde, in his evocative book *The Gift* (Hyde, 2007), devotes a whole chapter to the importance of "labour", as opposed to purely functional work, in honing creative gifts. He identifies the importance of structured approaches within which creativity can be given free play, and long time periods over which craft and skill can be honed, deepened and developed. Many creative practitioners (the term itself is instructive — creativity is part of a developed set of *practices*, not just a series of unconnected activities or transactions) would agree — while each practitioner's personal process might be unique, there is no denying that many have routines of some form to bring discipline to their creativity (Currey, 2013).

CONCLUSION

In some of the most famous lines in his magisterial *Four Quartets* — itself a paragon of creativity and poetic innovation — T. S. Eliot notes that "… last year's words belong to last year's language / And next year's words await another voice" (Eliot, 1962). Similarly, Singapore's efforts to be creative and innovative are likely to be a constant, iterative and experimental process, drawing equally on the richness of the metaphors of yesteryear, as well as new metaphors, with all the potential and possibilities they bring.

REFERENCES

Currey, M. (2013). *Daily routines: How great minds make time, find inspiration, and get to work.* London: Picador.

Eliot, T. S. (1962). *T. S. Eliot: The complete poems and plays, 1909–1950.* New York: Harcourt.

Hyde, L. (2007). *The gift: Creativity and the artist in the modern world* (2nd ed.). New York: Vintage Books.

Johansen, B. (2009). *Leaders make the future.* Oakland, Calif.: Berrett-Koehler.

Lakoff, G., & Johnson. M. (1980). *Metaphors we live by.* Chicago: University of Chicago Press.

Mauss, M. (1966). *The gift: Forms and functions of exchange in archaic societies* (I. Cunnison, Trans.) London: Cohen and West.

CHAPTER 6

What if Singapore Fails to Sustain Itself as a Vibrant, Cosmopolitan "Global City"?

AMANDA CHONG

THE "OUTSIDE-IN" VISION OF SINGAPORE AS A GLOBAL CITY

Since the founding of Singapore in 1819, our existence has been predicated on how attractive we are to the rest of the world. In 1819, it was our deep and sheltered harbour, our location at the crossroads of India and China in the zigzag of different trade routes. We drew immigrants from different countries and became a bustling port.

Post-independence, as we forged our own destiny, our attractiveness to the world became even more paramount. In 1972, it was declared that Singapore's very survival rested on our ability to become a "Global City" with the world as our hinterland (Rajaratnam, 1972). Singapore had to position itself as a haven for multinational corporations and foreign investors. Our tools of seduction? Political stability, law and order, a clean government.

In the 1990s, as we strove to shift our economy away from labour-intensive industries, it became clear that Singapore had to be attractive not just to corporations, we had to be attractive to people too. The right sort of people — global talent; the "creative class"; the class of knowledge workers who bring economic growth to the cities that they settle in (Florida, 2002). As Prime Minister (PM) Goh Chok Tong said in 1999, "We must make Singapore an oasis of talent. Many cities are vying to be the key global node in the region… who wins depends on who attracts the most talent, and forms a critical mass that draws in still more entrepreneurs, bankers, artists, writers, professionals" (Goh, 1999).

The creative class values diverse artistic and lifestyle experiences — we were going to provide them with that. A 1991 government report titled *The Next Lap* set the agenda: In order to attract global talent we must begin to nurture Singapore's creative and cultural sectors (Tan, 1998). This was never a priority in the earlier stages of our development; the founding prime minister, Lee Kuan Yew famously proclaimed that poetry was a luxury we could not afford. It was no secret that the economic imperative was the government's key driving force in cultivating the arts, as PM Goh put it in 1999: "Artistic creativity is an important element of a knowledge-based economy. [There will be] more funds to promote the arts" (Goh, 1999).

As we unpick this narrative, it becomes apparent that the vision of Singapore as a vibrant, cosmopolitan, global city is a vision built from the "outside-in". It is a branding exercise grounded in the desire to transform ourselves so we may be attractive to the world.

This vision has brought us many of the trappings of a cosmopolitan global city and indeed, the international reputation of being one. We host glittering events like the Formula 1 and ArtStage; we have built beautiful museums; government expenditure in the arts and cultural sector is approaching $700 million per year. As a result of these efforts and more, Singapore has been ranked as the best place in the world to live for expatriates — exactly what we had set out to achieve.

BUILDING SINGAPORE AS A GLOBAL CITY FROM THE "INSIDE-OUT"

When I think of Singapore in 2065, I am not worried that we will close our doors to the world and fail to sustain ourselves as a global, cosmopolitan city. We are far too pragmatic for that.

What I am concerned about is that if we continue in this trajectory of pursuing a vision of a global city built from the "outside-in" — while we may be opening our doors wide to the world, we may, ultimately, be closing the doors on ourselves.

As a poet and a member of Singapore's arts community, I want to focus on why, beyond attracting global talent, Singapore's arts scene is important for our own sake. The argument I want to advance is that the arts should not just or even primarily be an instrument of the state to attract global talent.

Instead of being a mere feature of the "outside-in" vision of Singapore as a global city, the arts can be an important part of Singapore's transformation into a mature and self-confident nation. In other words, the arts can be a vital way of constructing Singapore as a global city from the "inside-out". I propose three ways in which I believe that a more prominent role for the arts will help us to achieve this.

ART FORCES US TO ENGAGE WITH THE COMPLEXITY OF TRUTH

First, the arts help individuals come to grips with an increasingly complex world.

The world we live in today is highly polarised. We see this on our Facebook newsfeeds which have turned into echo-chambers. The Internet allows us to retreat into our own silos, interacting only with like-minded people who amplify our biases; we read only articles that re-inscribe our worldviews. At some point, we begin to feel no real need to engage with anyone with differing views. This impoverishes our national conversation.

Living in silos is intellectually easy. Reducing, simplifying and flattening issues allow us to preserve the instantaneous quality of our opinions. It saves us from the difficult but important work of consideration.

To be sure, many areas of human endeavour necessarily operate by simplifying and reducing. For example, the project of governance has to be reductionist to a certain degree. Singapore's own governance system relies on categorisation: first along the lines of race (the famous Chinese-Malay-Indian-Others, or "CMIO" model), then along the lines of religion, education and income. Categorisation is an indispensable tool for identifying problems and making policies. However, when categorisation entails oversimplification, especially of people, we must be mindful of the subtleties that are lost.

Art can develop that mindfulness, because art — or at least good art — does not traffic in reductionism. The arts, when unfettered by censorship, can give us the opportunity to engage with all shades of society and alternative views of life. Art can force us out of our silos, open up possibilities, and challenge us to consider a more complex version of the truth. The stage, novel and film are spaces in which we hear opinions from other than our own tribe. In his novel *The Last Lesson of Mrs de Souza*, Cyril Wong tells the story of a conservative school teacher who, compelled by a sense of moral responsibility, outs a gay boy to his own father resulting in devastating consequences. Wong's narrative is rich with ambivalence, forcing the reader to grapple with a complex issue.

Today, however, there is a sentiment within the arts community that the state only supports art which it deems "useful" for its instrumentalist goals. Singaporean artists feel that only art that steers clear of controversy is wholly embraced by the state. Works by Singapore artists that advance unorthodox political narratives have been censored or have had their funding withdrawn.

The graphic novel *The Art of Charlie Chan Hock Chye* by Sonny Liew is a famous example. In his book, Liew critically examines our political legacy and at one point, advances a counterfactual history of Lim Chin Siong as Singapore's first prime minister. His National Arts Council funding was pulled just a day before the book's launch. Still, his book went on to achieve critical acclaim, even making *The New York Times* bestsellers list — an unprecedented achievement that ought to have been cause for national celebration.

In order for art to perform the function of forcing us out of silos, we cannot embrace only art that entertains. We need art that challenges us. Such art can force us to see, hear and think differently, and ultimately decide for ourselves whether we want to act differently. Such art can also cultivate intellectual humility, or what the poet John Keats refers to as Negative Capability — the ability to live with uncertainty without irritably reaching for fact or reason. Such an openness of mind allows us to be poised to listen to one another so we may arrive at a more enriched version of the truth. Surely this is a hallmark of a mature society.

ART ENABLES US TO RECOGNISE OUR COMMON HUMANITY

Second, I believe art has an important role to play in Singapore because it enables us to recognise our common humanity. Former American President Barack Obama alluded to this when he revealed how literature was essential in keeping him focused on governance rather than politics. He said, "Fiction was useful as a reminder of the truths under the surface of what we argue about every day and was a way of seeing and hearing the voices, the multitudes of this country" (cited in Kakutani, 2017).

Art forces us into a place of receptivity, as we enlarge our universe and inhabit the lives of people of different genders, races, religions or political views. Art gives us a way of listening to voices that are not part of our daily lives. We are no longer cloistered in our narrow worlds, but are drawn out of ignorance into a place of empathy. Haresh Sharma's play *Off Centre* opened Singaporeans' eyes to the struggles of those with mental illness back in 1993 when "going to Woodbridge Hospital" was still a rude playground chide (Sharma, 2006).

More recently, some Singaporeans have angrily refused to have foreign worker dormitories in their own neighbourhoods, fearful that workers would soil their parks and cause public disturbances. Singapore's Ethos Books has published English translations of the poetry of Bangladeshi construction worker Md Mokul Hossine (Hossine, 2016). Mokul began scribbling poetry on cement bags at his construction site. His poetry challenges our close-minded stereotypes, and reminds us that we share a universal longing for home:

> Me migrant
> Live overseas
> Thousand thousand miles away
>
> …
>
> Me migrant
> Live outdoors
> Outside from you

Apart from giving us the opportunity to listen to the voices of others, the arts also enable us to see people as agents with layered motivations, who make meaningful choices based on their own values and expectations. This sense of empathy can inform the way we think about a myriad of topics including public policy.

As policymakers, we become less tempted to think of marginalised groups as objects to be acted upon or problems to be solved. But rather, a recognition of agency compels us to focus on building capacity and diminishing vulnerability in individuals. Instead of thinking how we can prescribe values, we focus on how we can empower individual decision-making. This can transform the way we think about policies to help those living in poverty, for example.

ART HELPS US RESOLVE SINGAPORE'S CRISIS OF STORY

Third and finally, the arts is important as a means of pondering new directions in the Singapore Story. The writer Gwee Li Sui says, "The central question Singapore is facing now, in the middle of the 2010s, is a crisis of story. It is a problem of what comes next, what kind of future to anticipate now that the declared goals of stability, prosperity and recognition are reached. This plight has been a long time coming" (Gwee, 2016).

The neatly defined arc of the Singapore Story — a sleepy fishing village transforming from Third World to First in a single generation — has long been completed. What narrative is there to replace it as we travel towards 2065? Conversations about what we value as a nation are now of utmost importance, and so is questioning the course that our country is on. These conversations may take place in conferences like this one, but they can also take place in the arts in a very powerful way.

We must be prepared for a multiplicity of voices to join in this conversation. What is good for our country cannot just be determined by politicians and policymakers. It has to be determined by the people too. The arts can be a valuable means for people to make sense of this question and to offer their own answers to it.

The arts is a realm in which an individual can inspect her inner world and a society can interrogate its own identity. This is the inherent value of culture. In every civilised society, it has long been the job of artists to ask difficult questions, and for those in power to listen. There may be uneasy truths that we need to hear, and dissenting voices that demand our consideration. One of the most notable voices is Alfian Sa'at. In his passionate poem *Singapore You are Not My Country* (Sa'at, 1998), he says:

> How can you call yourself a country, you terrible
> hallucination of highways and cranes and condominiums ten
> minutes' drive from the MRT?

We need look no further than the same poem to understand that dissent comes from a place of love, from an artist's sensitivity and concern for justice.

While his poem may appear to be a litany of accusations levelled at Singapore, Alfian ends the poem with this plaintive cry, which belies both a sense of dislocation and frustration at the limits of our historical consciousness:

> I have lost a country to images, it is as simple as that.
> Singapore you have a name on a map but no maps to your name.
> This will not do; we must stand aside and let the Lion crash
> through a madness of cymbals back to that darkjungle heart
> when eyes were still embers waiting for a crownless
> Prince of Palembang.

The surging popularity of Singapore poetry shows us that the arts is gaining special resonance in resolving our crisis of story. Every April over the past three years, more than 3,000 Singaporeans have gathered online to write a poem a day as part of Singapore Poetry Writing Month or "SingPoWriMo" (SingPoWriMo, n.d.). This group includes schoolboys, aunties and office-workers. They are writing not just in English but in inventive forms that sometimes even meld our four official languages.

The arts is a critical space in which our collective thoughts about Singapore are renewed. It is a way that society reiterates the ideals that are precious to us and protests the ones which need to be remade. As Singapore moves on from the project of survival to the project of building a legacy, the arts is a crucial way of visioning the country as we yearn it to be, of building a global city from the "inside out".

It is a way for us as Singaporeans to elevate our spirits and engage more deeply with the people around us. It is also a powerful indicator of how far we have come as a nation. This is the vision of a vibrant city we should sustain into 2065.

REFERENCES

Florida, R. (2002, May). The rise of the creative class. *The Washington Monthly*. Retrieved from: https://www.os3.nl/_media/2011-2012/richard_florida_-_the_rise_of_the_creative_class.pdf.

Goh, C. T. (1999, August 22). National Day Rally 1999. National Archives of Singapore. Retrieved from: http://www.nas.gov.sg/archivesonline/speeches/view-html?filename=1999082202.htm.

Gwee, L. S. (2016). Foreword. In Chia, C., Ip, J., & Lee, C. J. (Eds.), *A luxury we must afford* (pp. 17–20). Singapore: Math Paper Press.

Hossine, M. M. (2016). *Me migrant*. Singapore: Ethos Books.

Kakutani, M. (2017, January 16). Transcript: President Obama on what books mean to him. *The New York Times*. Retrieved from: https://www.nytimes.com/2017/01/16/books/transcript-president-obama-on-what-books-mean-to-him.html.

Liew, S. (2015). *The art of Charlie Chan Hock Chye*. Singapore: Epigram Books.

Rajaratnam, S. (1972, February 6). Address by S. Rajaratnam to the Singapore Press Club. National Archives of Singapore. Retrieved from: http://www.nas.gov.sg/archivesonline/data/pdfdoc/PressR19720206a.pdf.

Sa'at, A. B. (1998). *One fierce hour*. Singapore: Landmark Books.

Sharma, H. (2006). *Off centre*. Singapore: One Play Series.

SingPoWriMo. (n.d.). In *Facebook* [Group page]. Retrieved from: https://www.facebook.com/groups/singpowrimo/.

Tan, L. Y. (1998). *Singapore: The next lap*. Singapore: Times Editions for the Government of Singapore.

Wong, C. (2013). *The last lesson of Mrs de Souza*. Singapore: Epigram Books.

SECTION **III**

Looking Across

CHAPTER 7

What if We Ignore Race and Religion?

NORMAN VASU AND PRAVIN PRAKASH

The exchange between Nominated Member of Parliament (NMP) Viswa Sadasivan and the late Minister Mentor Lee Kuan Yew in Parliament back in 2009 clearly illustrates the two different ways race and religion is understood in Singapore. In his maiden parliamentary speech, Sadasivan called for a return to the much cherished words of Singapore's National Pledge, "one united people, regardless of race, language and religion" as a "core belief system" and "a set of inalienable values" that "demands adherence in the face of the lure of pragmatism". He further argued that while it was challenging to unite people of diverse cultural backgrounds, Singapore should never stop trying to fashion a "collective reflex" (Parliament of Singapore, 2009a). The speech raised a strong response, with Lee saying that he wished to "bring the House back to earth". Arguing that the NMP's words were "false and flawed", he said it was "dangerous to allow such highfalutin ideas to go undemolished and mislead Singapore" (Parliament of Singapore, 2009b).

It is clear from the exchange that the understanding of religious and race relations in Singapore have essentially existed in two distinct camps. The first and perhaps more dominant camp — expressed by Lee — is one founded upon an essentialist understanding of identity — one where identities are viewed as primordial and immutable. From this perspective, Singaporeans coming from diverse ethnic and cultural backgrounds will irrevocably retain a sense of being different. As such, while it is critical to focus on building an intercommunal, core Singaporean identity, citizens' full sense of identity will permanently exist in a state of hyphenation — a Singaporean-something. Informed by the communal violence of the past, this view stresses the need to be grounded in the realities of communal identities and it demands an appreciation of the fragility of ethnic relations in Singapore.

The second camp often finds its legitimacy in the much cherished words of the Pledge — the normative goal of becoming "one united people, regardless of race, language or religion." It views ethnic and cultural identities as non-essentialist and mutable. Members of this camp believe ethnic and cultural identities can be altered and shaped, thereby permitting the creation of a Singaporean identity strong enough to exist *sans* hyphenation. The second camp, however, has often been dismissed as being quixotic and lacking practical relevance. Echoing this view in his National Day Rally in 2016, Prime Minister (PM) Lee Hsien Loong referred to the findings of the study conducted that year by Channel NewsAsia (CNA) and the Institute of Policy Studies (IPS) and said "race does matter, and will matter for a long time to come" when Singaporeans make a full range of decisions — from the personal to the political (Lee, 2016).

Dismissing the second camp has led to a peculiar phenomenon in Singapore. In the absence of "highfalutin" ideals, an essentialist understanding of communal identity has led to a focus on passing strong legislation to ensure racial harmony is maintained and the worst outcome that communal difference may bring is avoided. The view has also enshrined the critical and central role the state plays in the management of ethnicity and religion in Singapore and has also entrenched a strong belief that policy-making aimed at managing such a powder keg must be drenched thoroughly in pragmatism.

The dominance of pragmatism and the ingrained perspective of primordial identities dictate that ignoring race and religion will remain a "highfalutin" ideal. However, pragmatism also dictates that policies and perspectives change with time, context and normative goals. As such, it may be prudent that Singapore reflects upon how its approach to the management of its multicultural complexion can evolve with growing diversity and changing times. Is there a different approach that can be taken to manage communal relations in Singapore come 2065? What is the Singapore that Singaporeans would like to see? In this contribution, two alternatives to the current approach to managing race and religion in Singapore are explored and readers are left to decide which he or she prefers or might wish to be committed to. It does so in three sections. The first section discusses Singapore's current model of managing race and religion in Singapore. The second section then introduces the first alternative to the current model — customarily termed "soft multiculturalism" in academic literature — and is one that demands revolutionary change to the current approach. Finally, the third section discusses the second alternative termed the "Singapore-plus model" that offers an evolution of the current approach.

THE CURRENT SINGAPOREAN SYSTEM — HARD MULTICULTURALISM AND MUSCULAR SECULARISM

As indicated earlier, it is undeniable that Singapore's approach to the management of race and religion is undoubtedly one of hard multiculturalism. Hard multiculturalism maintains that the very purpose of politics is to manage group difference (Miller, 1995). It is an approach more commonly associated with communitarians such as Charles Taylor and Will Kymlicka (Kymlicka, 1996; see also Taylor & Gutmann, 1994). A general feature of hard multiculturalism is that the state acts in the central role of manager, protector and if needed, arbitrator between different cultural groups. Motivated by the belief that cultural identity is the key enabling tool through which people understand the world, the position distinguishes itself from other approaches by being openly supportive of state intervention to protect cultural differences (Taylor & Gutmann, 1994). It is important to note that under hard multiculturalism, cultural differences cannot influence the manner in which, for example, *habeas corpus* is determined, but a polity should be allowed to "weigh the importance of the uniform treatment of individuals against the importance of cultural survival, and opt sometimes in the favour of the latter" (p. 61). Following from this, hard multiculturalism protects group rights through the institutional recognition of cultural difference in the public sphere in areas such as, political representation.

With regard to Singapore, its policy is indisputably one of hard multiculturalism. At its founding in 1965, Singapore embraced multiracialism as its official multicultural policy with differences within the new nation administratively limited to the racial boxes of Chinese, Malay, Indian and Others (CMIO). Largely inherited from census-taking in the British colonial period, this racial categorisation reflects the two major sources of immigration to the island when the British first established a trading post here — China and South Asians from British India — along with a recognition of the indigenous people on the island and in the immediate Southeast Asia region. The immigrant Chinese soon developed into the majority, and by the 1960s, they already comprised 65 percent of the population. At political independence, the national demographic distribution stood at 75 percent ethnic Chinese, 17 percent Malays, 7 percent Indians, and a small percentage of "Others" — individuals who were not considered Chinese, Malay or Indian by the state were, by process of elimination, defined as being in the "Other" category. Typically, they would include the Eurasians and Jews.

Therefore, the Singaporean model of hard multiculturalism has been founded on an immutable understanding of race where individuals are recognised to have only one unchanging racial identity. To preserve the racial boundaries of the CMIO categories, the Singaporean state enforces a strict bureaucratic separation among the groups by determining a citizen's race by paternal line. This ascribed racial category is recorded in one's birth certificate and national identity card. The possibility of altering the ascribed racial identity or expanding the four categories to better reflect mixed cultural parentage is limited. In recent years, Singapore has admittedly loosened the requirement for race to be defined by paternal line. Bi-racial children are permitted to reflect their bi-racial status with a hyphenated racial identity. However, in dealings with the state, the race appearing before the hyphen is considered the child's "prime" race.[1] For example, a Malay-Chinese individual will be treated as Malay by the state.

In such a system of managing diversity, that management goes beyond ascription as it has to take place in a "lived" identificational container. The state does this in various ways. Besides administrative enforcement of the racial categories, the state has also essentialised the cultural identities of each race by furnishing these races with "unique" cultural traits — suggesting in

---

[1] For more information, refer to Singapore Immigration and Checkpoints Authority (2010).

many forms of public communications that language, dress, food and the arts are distinct and associated with one of the four racial groups. Moreover, these cultural traits are held to be permanent and are passed down through the generations. This essentialisation of race through these markers is most clearly expressed in the celebration of "Racial Harmony Day" in Singapore's schools on July 21. Students are made to dress, eat and dance in the "traditional" manner of their ascribed culture in an effort to, as noted by PM Lee, "celebrate our diversity, and share each other's customs and cultures" and drive home the idea that "harmony between our different races and religions is a fundamental principle of our nation" (Nair, 2016).

Beyond the preservation of racial boundaries through administrative diktat as well as the investment of unique traits, other government policies pertaining to education, housing, the electoral system and socio-economic assistance further reinforce racial distinctions among Singaporeans.

With regard to education, while the language of instruction is English, since the 1980s, students have been required to study their "mother-tongue" — a misnomer for a policy that up to now, demands they study a second language associated with the race following their paternal line. As such, the Chinese learn Mandarin, the Malays learn the Malay language and the Indians — recognising the greater linguistic variation within South Asian communities — Bengali, Gujarati, Hindi, Punjabi or Urdu.

Besides education, Singapore's housing policy further amplifies racial distinction with the imposition of racial quotas since 1989 which aims to prevent the emergence of racial enclaves in a country where approximately 83 percent of the population live in government-built housing estates. Hence, having created "hard" racial distinctions in the public sphere, the Singaporean government has subsequently been forced to impinge upon the housing market to ensure the constructed racial groups do not constellate together.

In 1988, the need to manage the CMIO categories spilled over into the political arena. Singapore practises a variant of British parliamentary democracy and, in order to ensure that the non-Chinese minority in Singapore will consistently have parliamentary representation, some constituencies have become Group Representation Constituencies (GRCs). Within a GRC, a team of politicians represents a constituency and the members of the team have to include at least one non-minority candidate, the race of which is specified by the President on the advice of the Cabinet. In 2016, the government also passed constitutional amendments to ensure all races are represented in the office of the Elected President (EP) as Head of State from time to time by stipulating that an election will be reserved for a racial group if they have not been represented for five continuous terms (Yong, 2016).

Finally, with regard to socio-economic aid, the Singaporean government established in 1982, a precedent for the development of racial self-help groups by setting up the Development of Singapore Malay/Muslim Community (MENDAKI) charged with finding solutions to social issues such as drug abuse, teenage pregnancy and educational under-achievement.

The management of religion in Singapore has also closely mirrored the concept of hard multiculturalism in enshrining the centrality and active participation of the state. Ramakrishna refers to Singapore's approach towards managing religion as "muscular secularism", noting the state's "no-nonsense position on religion" and its presence as a "neutral umpire between the contending interests of the various faiths" (Ramakrishna, 2010, p. 9–10). Abdullah refers to muscular secularism as "a direct, interventionist approach" to ensure "the submission of religion to the overarching authority of the state, rendering the state the final arbiter in all affairs within its borders (Abdullah, 2013). Tan highlights that the Singapore state "is deeply involved in, concerned with and exerts a measured influence over religious matters" and organisations (Tan, 2008). This is to ensure that "religion does not cross over to the political domain" and can be observed in the state exerting a "symbolic and putative influence on the administration of faiths subscribed to by Singapore's racial minorities, viz. Islam, Sikhism and Hinduism" (Tan, 2008). Tan also argues that Singapore "adopts a calibrated mixture of hard and soft law" in regulating and controlling religious groups which attempts to "ensure that the laws generate norms and behaviour that become self-enforcing" (Tan, 2009). Like race, religion is carefully defined, packaged and managed through active state intervention to ensure that multicultural harmony is maintained.

MILD MULTICULTURALISM — BENIGN NEGLECT

"Mild multiculturalism", while acknowledging the diversity of cultures within a polity, holds that the business of states does not extend into cultural matters. Instead, cultural diversity is recognised as part of the private sphere. For such a state, which is neutral towards questions of cultural diversity, the only assimilation expected from all its members is that they accept the idea of the neutral state in the public sphere. Therefore, a degree of assimilation is expected of immigrants and ethnic minorities in the public sphere of law and government, the market, education, and employment. The assimilation demanded of all members of the polity is an acceptance of the liberal political culture that enables the state to practise a policy of "benign neglect" with regard to communal difference (Kukathas, 1997) — a neglect allowing a polity to be "an association of individuals and groups living under the rule of law but pursuing separate ends or purposes."[2] An example often cited for the practice of mild multiculturalism would be the United States (US) where the state, though acknowledging its populace to be composed of different cultural communities, does not guarantee the survival of their individual cultures. Hence, for example, although the US acknowledges its Italian American community, it does not actively play a role in ensuring the survival of Italian American culture.

This form of multiculturalism has been defended by some of the more prominent liberal philosophers in contemporary times including Ronald Dworkin and John Rawls (Rawls, 1971; see also Dworkin, 1979). This position acknowledges that different people have different conceptions of the good life. As there can be no way to discern who has the correct conception, there is a commitment to treat everyone fairly and equally, regardless of how one perceives the good life. The commitment to treat everyone equally and fairly has led others to refer to such a position as "procedural". The role of the state is limited to ensuring equal respect whilst it does not propound any one perfect conception of the good life (Taylor & Gutmann, 1994, p. 56). Thus, the policy of multiculturalism in this mild form emerges from the legally protected autonomy of the individual by the

---

[2] Admittedly, the word *neutral* here may be misleading, as no society is strictly neutral. All political institutions have a historical character that prevents them from being strictly neutral. For example, political institutions shaped by European traditions tend to produce governments and laws that are more likely to be conducted and written in a European language, their parliaments will betray some European influences in procedure, and they may celebrate certain holidays. For more information, refer to Kukathas (1998, p. 697).

state. The state deals equally with all, and the citizens deal fairly with each other. A facet of this form of multiculturalism is that the state guarantees a broad spectrum of cultural identities but it does not guarantee the survival of any. Intervention by the state to ensure the survival of specific cultural groups would run counter to its stance on remaining neutral.

In recent decades, there has been a rising call for this milder form of multiculturalism in Singapore — one with a reduced presence of the state in directing communal issues; allowing communities and individuals to organise and negotiate issues of cultural identity without its intervention. An argument commonly articulated is that the state in Singapore must relinquish socio-political space to stimulate a naturally-evolved communal identity and civil society must accept its multicultural composition and possess the maturity to navigate potential cultural tensions without need for government involvement (Ramakrishna, 2010, p. 15–17). These advocates contend that a more modern cosmopolitan Singaporean citizenry "despite their diverse faith and ethnic backgrounds, are well able to display the necessary political and emotional maturity to exercise rational judgement" when confronted with issues of race and religion (Ramakrishna, 2010, p. 15–17).

This has been observed most often in the periodic debates involving the CMIO model with critics claiming the model is increasingly archaic and irrelevant, out of touch with the increasing diversity of Singapore's population, and counter-productive to the cohesion of a multicultural population 50 years down the road in terms of fashioning a collective independent identity. Sadasivan, suggesting in 2015 that there be a "review and recalibration" of the CMIO, argued that as Singapore "matures to look past cultural and religious differences, CMIO could become a crutch that holds back progress towards multiculturalism" (Sadasivan, 2016). Indeed it has been noted by sociologists that "the CMIO model is potentially constraining as it pigeonholes people and, to a certain extent perpetuates racial stereotypes" by creating "expectations of how to fulfil one's identity" in line with one's prescribed racial category (Sim, 2015).

Similar arguments have been made with regard to the management of religion and secularism in Singapore. Putting forward the idea that the Singaporean populace is increasingly mature, educated, and attuned to the sensitivities of a multicultural setting, advocates argue for the state to "do away with its paternalist attitude towards governance" and "trust Singaporeans to do the right thing" in the public sphere and civil society to regulate and steer itself (Ramakrishna, 2010, p.15–17). This concept of "liberal secularism" contends that "the form of religious tolerance that ensues from state interference is a superficial, if not artificial one, while a bottom-up form of tolerance, which will occur as a result of liberal secularism, is the real, lasting form" (Abdullah, 2013). The Association of Women for Action and Research (AWARE) saga of 2009, which saw an attempt by a conservative Christian group to take over the organisation and the subsequent mobilisation and removal of this group by more liberal sections of the group, through completely constitutional means and without the presence or interference of the government, is often extolled as an example of the public sphere's capacity to contend, contest and calibrate itself without need for state intervention.

Undeniably, there are several arguments that make the case for the Singaporean state to embrace mild multiculturalism. However, the familiar well-worn retort from the oppositional camp is to brand such arguments as being neither practical nor pragmatic. As articulated above, race and religion continue to be viewed as primordial essentialist cultural cleavages that could fracture the national fabric. This essentialised view leads to the belief that communal identities have to be managed and cannot be overcome. Events of recent years are highlighted to support it. The sobering reality of "insider threats" incubating within Singapore unearthed by the Internal Security Department (ISD), as well as the presence of a plot to fire a rocket into Singapore from Batam have indicated that cultural identities continue to be combustible commodities and that security threats remain very real (*Today*, 2016). In January 2016, Home Affairs and Law Minister K. Shanmugam articulated the narrative of an increasingly "somewhat distant" Muslim population and the threat of heightened Islamophobia within the population (CNA, 2016). Analysts have referred to this as increasing "social distance", and it is recognised to be a natural side-effect of the greater phenomenon of a collision between cultural globalisation and traditional cultural identities (Ramakrishna, 2016). It has also been articulated that a key feature of increased social distance is the creation of enclaves with communities increasingly insulating themselves from one another (Ramakrishna, 2016).

Global political trends, too, seem to indicate that the current historical epoch may be one of cultural tensions. Communal identities have grown increasingly complex and difficult to label, with racism, religious extremism and xenophobia becoming an unwelcome hydra of negativity and cynicism. Recent global events such as Brexit where the voters in the United Kingdom opted to leave the European Union, the election of an anti-immigrant Donald Trump to the presidency in the US elections, the rise of Hindutva in Indian politics, the increasing communal tone of politics in both Indonesia and Malaysia all suggest that a shift from a careful management of multiculturalism in Singapore would be impractical and not in line with the pragmatic mould of Singapore public policymaking.[3]

THE SINGAPORE-PLUS MODEL

The discussions in the preceding sections lead us to certain observations about multiculturalism in Singapore and its foreseeable and preferable future. It can be observed that the prospect of ignoring race and religion and pursuing a Singapore identity *sans* hyphenation will be perceived as too quixotic, idealistic and utopian. It is also clear that the state can conceivably continue to play a major role, if not a dominant one in the management of multiculturalism as we look towards the future. Furthermore, any shift in our multicultural policy framework may have to be evolutionary rather than revolutionary — one which evolves from the current model of multiculturalism in Singapore that has helped so much in ensuring multicultural harmony and preventing cultural conflict. Arguably, this is attributable to the primacy of pragmatism as a guiding philosophy that shapes our approach towards both multiculturalism and policymaking in Singapore. Pragmatism has served Singapore well with regard to intercommunal relations. How can pragmatism further improve Singapore's sterling record of intercommunal relations in the future?

An evolution as opposed to a revolution may be an option here. A pragmatic evolution to the policy of multiculturalism here would be to

---

[3] This position has been stated repeatedly by the political leadership in Singapore recently, most notably by Minister K. Shanmugam at a recent symposium. For more information, refer to "Singapore must safeguard position of minorities amid growing polarisation abroad: Shanmugam" (Salleh, 2017).

work with the current CMIO framework and evolve it towards achieving desirable outcomes of representation, knowledge-building, integration, and capacity-building. The "Singapore-plus" alternative suggests that while pragmatism has served Singapore's multiculturalism well, it can be better employed with greater consistency towards the enhancement of multicultural harmony in Singapore. Pragmatism is rooted in the idea that all endeavour has to have a clear goal and the means chosen to achieve it should be decided upon by the efficiency or effectiveness of doing that. As noted, Singapore, in general, has a strong sense of the kind of society it does not want and guards against that with a watchful state apparatus and strong laws. However it is debatable if there is a clear practical consensus on the quality of multiculturalism desired. If racial or religious riots are the extreme scenarios Singapore wants to avoid, if a utopian commonality with no conflict is impossible, and if the different communal communities of Singapore have to continue to live cheek by jowl in peace, what is the world that is slightly below the level of utopia that the polity can aspire to? Keeping in mind that the key to the successful application of pragmatism as a decision-making methodology is goal-setting followed by a decision on the best way by which to achieve that goal, it is puzzling Singapore sets for itself few clear targets on how it would like to see the pragmatic endgame, target or *telos* for the quality of multicultural relations. This inconsistent application of pragmatism's decision-making methodology may have to be addressed for Singapore to improve upon the already sturdy state of inter-racial relations achieved.

Target-setting for the quality of multiculturalism in Singapore will bring significant benefits. Firstly, the setting of achievable goals would offer clear key performance indicators on whether progress is being made in the right direction or if there are deficits that must be remedied. Secondly, it will also permit better understanding of the data collected on the state of inter-racial relations. In the CNA-IPS Survey cited earlier, 40 percent of the respondents reported that their close friends were at least mildly racist (Mathews, 2016). To make sense of whether this is an alarming finding, a benchmark is needed. Lastly, the process of setting such targets will require Singaporeans to have a national conversation and work towards a consensus on targets they feel is achievable multicultural harmony for the future. If the version of multiculturalism expressed in the Pledge is purely aspirational, then what is the firm achievable goal in multicultural harmony that we can hope to arrive at which is a step below that?

Singapore's approach to ensuring minority representation in Parliament though GRCs as well as the new system of reserved elections for the EP system is highly instructive here. While it would seem impractical to set a goal of say ensuring that in the next survey, only 20 percent of the respondents as opposed to 40 percent say that their close friends are mildly racist, it may be possible to set goals where the racial profile of people in each occupation or those with specific educational qualifications represent the demographic breakdown of Singapore society by race. An example here would be the goal of having the number of doctors in Singapore reflect the racial demographic of the nation by year X. Or perhaps by year X, those possessing university degrees should reflect the racial demographic of the country.

It should be emphasised that the argument put forward here is not a call for quotas or for affirmative action where the unqualified are lifted unfairly above their abilities or for exam grades to be fudged. Rather, it is to establish targets and clear goals to be achieved in a given number of years. Quotas and affirmative action are focused on fixing outcomes rather than structural issues. Targets focus the mind on dealing with the structural issues to arrive at the desired outcome.

As such, exactly like the proposed amendments to the EP system, individuals will have to meet the high standards demanded by such occupations for entry and students are assessed uniformly. Eschewing affirmative action of quotas through the proposed, the state instead devotes its energy to help under-represented races in particular occupations or the educationally underperforming races rise to the standards to attain the goals set. Along with the state, organisations, institutions and industries where these targets have been set will have to function as equal partners to achieve them. The state may offer incentives to do so. This may stimulate research and development initiatives that build capacity to achieve the targets. Crucially, it will enable society and the private sector to become stakeholders in the normative agenda of multiculturalism.

Some may argue against what is proposed by asking about the utility of achieving those goals. How would having occupations or educational attainment reflect the racial demographic of Singapore improve the quality of inter-racial relations? This is a fair question easily answered. Just as the underlying rationale for making adjustments to the EP is based on the utility of having the presidency reflect the multiracial tapestry of Singapore, all other occupations arguably should too. The benefits are psychological and inspirational. Singaporeans from different cultural backgrounds would be able to look at and, more importantly, experience Singaporean life as it is — a rainbow of phenotypic hues and religion, reflective of reality whatever the sphere of interaction; a place where one can be anything one strives for based on a system of culturally vigilant and sensitive meritocracy. Rather than ignoring race and religion, or viewing such a shift as being impractical, the current framework can evolve to target structural issues that can foster greater multicultural unity. Surely such an approach would be both pragmatic and satisfyingly Singaporean.

CONCLUSION

What would the management of Singapore's multicultural constitution look like in 2065? The truthful answer is no one knows. The twin variables of the imperatives of the particular temporal moment and the dominant understanding of the present as well as past are far too capricious to formulate a definitive, believable conclusion. Undoubtedly many will try but perhaps the best suggestions and projections should be founded upon clearly expressed premises with regard to how communal identity is understood and what a normative proposition that is coherent with such a premise is. It is hoped that this contribution has offered a starting point for a robust conversation about the management of Singapore's multicultural future.

REFERENCES

Abdullah, W. J. (2013). Religious representation in secular Singapore: A case study of MUIS and Pergas. *Asian Survey, 53*(6), 1182–1204.

Channel NewsAsia. (2016, January 19). Singapore must do more to safeguard racial, religious harmony: Shanmugam. Retrieved from: http://www.channelnewsasia.com/news/singapore/Singapore-must-do-more-to/2438094.html.

Dworkin, R. (1979). *Taking rights seriously*. London: Duckworth.

Kukathas, C. (1997). Multiculturalism as fairness: Will Kymlicka's multicultural citizenship. *Journal of Political Philosophy*, 5(4), 423–24.

Kukathas, C. (1998). Liberalism and multiculturalism: The politics of indifference. *Political Theory*, 26(5), 686–699.

Kymlicka, W. (1996). *Multicultural citizenship*. New York: Oxford University Press.

Lee, H. L. (2016, August 21). National Day Rally 2016. Prime Minister's Office. Retrieved from: http://www.pmo.gov.sg/national-day-rally-2016.

Mathews, M. (2016). Key findings from the Channel NewsAsia-Institute of Policy Studies survey on race relations. Retrieved from: http://lkyspp.nus.edu.sg/ips/wp-content/uploads/sites/2/2013/04/CNA-IPS-survey-on-race-relations_Summary.

Miller, D. (1995). *On nationality*. Oxford: Clarendon Press.

Nair, S. (2016, July 21). Harmony between different races and religions fundamental for Singapore: PM Lee. *The Straits Times*. Retrieved from: http://www.straitstimes.com/singapore/harmony-between-different-races-and-religions-fundamental-for-singapore-pm-lee.

Parliament of Singapore. (2009a, August 18). Singapore parliamentary report. *Parliamentary Debates (Hansard) Vol. 86*. Retrieved from: http://sprs.parl.gov.sg/search/report.jsp?currentPubID=00004791-WA.

Parliament of Singapore. (2009b, August 19). Singapore parliamentary report. *Parliamentary Debates (Hansard) Vol. 86*. Retrieved from: http://sprs.parl.gov.sg/search/report.jsp?currentPubID=00075281-ZZ.

Ramakrishna, K. (2010). "Muscular" versus "liberal" secularism and the religious fundamentalist challenge in Singapore. *RSIS Working Paper* (no. 22), 9–17.

Ramakrishna, K. (2016, February 1). Religious fundamentalism and social distancing: Cause for concern? *RSIS Commentary*. Retrieved from: https://www.rsis.edu.sg/rsis-publication/rsis/co023-religious-fundamentalism-and-social-distancing-cause-for-concern/#.WaVAuMgjEfk.

Rawls, J. (1971). *A theory of justice.* Cambridge, MA: Harvard University Press.

Sadasivan, V. (2016, September 8). CMIO — Is it time to de-emphasise it? Population.sg. Retrieved from: https://www.population.sg/articles/cmio--is-it-time-to-deemphasise-it.

Salleh, N. A. M. (2017, February 1). Singapore must safeguard position of minorities amid growing polarisation abroad: Shanmugam. *The Straits Times.* Retrieved from: http://www.straitstimes.com/singapore/singapore-must-safeguard-position-of-minorities-amid-growing-polarisation-abroad-shanmugam.

Sim, W. (2015, November 8). Race categorisation too rigid for increasingly diverse S'pore? *The Straits Times.* Retrieved from: http://www.straitstimes.com/politics/race-categorisation-too-rigid-for-increasingly-diverse-spore.

Singapore Immigration and Checkpoints Authority. (2010, December 29). Public advisory: Greater flexibility with implementation of double-barrelled race option from 1 January 2011. Retrieved from: http://www.ica.gov.sg/news_details.aspx?nid=12443.

Tan, E. K. (2008). Keeping god in place: The management of religion. In Lai, A. E. (Ed.), *Religious diversity in Singapore,* pp. 66–68. Singapore: ISEAS.

Tan, E. K. (2009). From clampdown to limited empowerment: Soft law in the calibration and regulation of religious conduct in Singapore. *Law & Policy, 31*(3), 351–379.

Taylor, C., & Gutmann, A. (1994). *Multiculturalism: Examining the politics of recognition.* Princeton: Princeton University Press.

Today. (2016, August 5). Singapore on alert after 6 terror suspects arrested in Batam over rockets plot. Retrieved from: http://www.todayonline.com/singapore/6-terror-suspects-arrested-plotting-hit-marina-bay-rocket-batam-reports.

Yong, C. (2016, November 10). Parliament passes changes to elected presidency. *The Straits Times.* Retrieved from: http://www.straitstimes.com/singapore/parliament-passes-changes-to-presidency.

CHAPTER 8

What if We Cease to Accept Immigrants?

MARIAM JAAFAR

FOUR TRENDS SHAPING SINGAPORE'S SOCIO-ECONOMIC OUTLOOK

What if Singapore were to cease accepting immigrants? Perhaps the unsatisfactory answer is: It depends.

This is a difficult question to answer. It depends partly on global trends that are beyond our control, and partly on some things that are within our control, like our public policy responses and our achievements together as a nation.

What makes it most interesting is that the things that are beyond our control are further complicated by the unprecedented level of uncertainty that the world faces today. Let me identify four big uncertainties that we know something about, and leave room for readers to consider the breadth of what we do not yet know.

The first factor we must consider is an obvious one — technology. Today, prototypes already exist for self-driving cars, robotic garbage collectors and doctors that are really just artificial intelligence (AI) at work, and exoskeleton suits. There is still a lot of uncertainty over how this new wave of automation technologies like AI, robotics and big data will play out.

Take for example, general artificial intelligence, the holy grail of AI. The experts say this may be 20 years out, or it may be even 150 years out. The problem is that big spread or range. Much of the conversation today is about how technology will take away a significant number of jobs, both blue and white collar jobs, with some estimates saying 47 percent of the jobs that exist today will be replaced by it.

Indeed, many of the activities that we do today will become obsolete, including many of the labour-intensive tasks that are being done by immigrants and migrant workers in Singapore. We also hear that some jobs will be transformed because these new tools will make humans more productive rather than replace them. Of course, there will be new jobs that are created because of these technological developments. The question is exactly what those jobs will be — the ones that are transformed; newly created; how many will there be; when will they come? How can we know the future?

We do know that technological developments will have a huge impact on how we think about jobs for Singapore residents and immigrants.

Second, the global economy. The question here is: Will globalisation and international cooperation pick up from here? Or will it regress to protectionism over the next 50 years?

Third, the social developments that arise from the first two points: Will income inequality continue to grow or will we find a path to inclusive growth?

Fourth, the political impact and the question is: Will polarisation, this disturbing trend we see today, continue to take root? Or can we actually rebuild trust so that we can become more cohesive again and go back to the politics of "We"?

So, those are four big uncertainties: technology, globalisation, income inequality, and political divisiveness. Which way we go depends not only on globalisation and technology, but institutions, policies and the politics that the big economies of the world engage in. As a small city-state, Singapore is highly exposed to these uncertainties. Our domestic public policy response and how we adapt will be critical factors.

Take the two by two matrix that you see on the next page, where the y-axis denotes the march of technology and the x-axis denotes the social, political and economic adaptations — on the right you have progressive, integrated, and inclusive development, and on the left, you have regressive, divided and unequal development. We can work out some scenarios of Singapore's future based on how the key uncertainties discussed earlier interact with each other.

What if We Cease to Accept Immigrants?

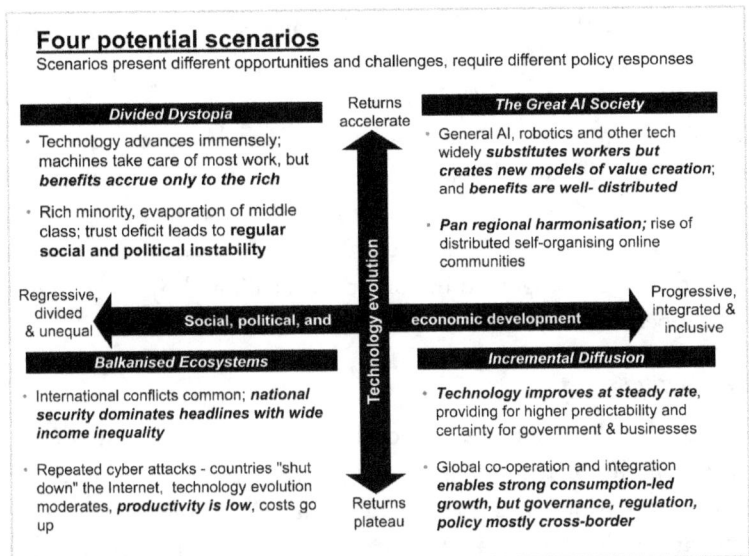

The Great AI Society

In the top right corner, you get the "Great AI Society". This is where technology has advanced to the point where it has created an increase in productivity and a rise in new business opportunities. General AI and robotics have become pervasive, and will probably replace human workers in many activities.

New models of value creation have emerged in this advanced digital economy, where the marginal cost of production is low or near zero. The economic adjustments from displacements have been made and the benefits are equitably distributed, allowing prosperous, sustainable, and long lives for all of us.

Talent, capital, ideas are fully mobile across national boundaries. Like the utopia in H. G. Wells' novel *Men Like Gods*, the concept of the nation-state has weakened with the rise of decentralised, self-organising communities that transcend national boundaries.

Incremental Diffusion

What if you do not get the discontinuities in technology that are discussed in the first scenario, the Great AI Society? Well, you have the "Incremental Diffusion" scenario, or what I call my "Back to the Future" scenario, because you will still have those hoverboards you watched in that 1985 *Back to the Future* movie presented by Steven Spielberg.

Technology allows a gradual increase in automation and software tools that support people in their day-to-day work, and improve quality of life. However, the slower pace of change here compared to the first scenario helps to create better predictability and certainty for governments and businesses to plan the future. Globalisation has continued, goods, capital, talent are fully mobile, and that exchange and interaction is facilitated by regional and pan-regional cooperation.

Divided Dystopia

On the top left side of the matrix, you have what I call "Divided Dystopia". Here, the benefits of technology are significant but they have entrenched power in corporations and the wealthy elite. Machines have pushed the majority into joblessness and poverty. The middle class is gone. Economic and digital divides have led to regular social disturbances and toppled many governments around the world, causing people to turn inwards and put up barriers to globalisation and trade.

Balkanised Ecosystems

Finally, on the bottom right is the fourth scenario I call "Balkanised Ecosystem". This is an Orwellian future where the world is in a state of perpetual conflict, and all forms of economic and political unions that we know of, have broken down. The European Union is no more, free trade agreements between countries and across regions have all been ripped up. Recurring cyber-attacks have caused governments to restrict the Internet, moderating the advance of technology. Productivity is low, and the general standard of living is lower such that consumer goods are scarce and expensive; they are available mostly to the upper classes in an unequal society.

Each of these scenarios presents different opportunities and challenges, requiring different policy responses. How we respond to them could lead to very different national outcomes. For example, in the Great AI Society, if we close our doors to the best, most highly-skilled talent and entrepreneurs who are going to create these new innovations, it is likely that we will fall behind because they will go somewhere else; they are free to go wherever they want, to whichever country that welcomes them. On the other hand, if we go out to attract and retain the best of them, perhaps the next Google might have its origins in Singapore.

Clearly, when I refer to the best global talent, I mean both Singaporeans and foreigners. Also, as the concept of the nation-state weakens, how you build that connection back to your diaspora becomes really important and that is an opportunity for us — to tap Singaporean talent that has been based overseas till now.

On the lower end of the labour market, it does not really matter whether we choose to accept immigrants or not. If there are no jobs, they will not be headed here anyway. In this scenario, if there were a blanket restriction on immigration, it would probably lead to Singapore losing competitiveness and the outcome would be sub-par growth.

This is a long way to explain why I say that the answer to what might happen if Singapore were to cease accepting immigrants is that "it depends"; it depends on how these scenarios play out, and what our domestic policy responses will be. The impact will be on the growth of the economy, jobs, as well as the level of well-being of Singaporeans more generally.

THE KEY PREMISE OF ECONOMIC GROWTH

I think it is important to clarify we are operating on one key premise — the premise that economic growth depends on immigration and that growth matters at all. Why does economic growth matter?

There are indeed many non-economic indicators that matter in ascertaining a country's progress and well-being. My firm, for example, the Boston Consulting Group, has a sustainable economic development assessment framework, and it tracks 43 different indicators and not all of them are economic ones.

So while it is true that growth is not all that matters, it is also true that growth does matter. With global growth being so anaemic today, I think one will accept that growth matters a little bit more. You need growth to keep up with inflation, and you also need growth to, more importantly, give opportunities and hope to everyone such as businesses, but also the young so that they can believe their lives will improve over time.

Singapore no longer enjoys exceptional growth rates. We are not talking about the difference between an economic growth rate of 6 percent and

7 percent a year. We are talking about the difference between achieving a 2 percent or 3 percent increase or perhaps even just 1 percent and 2 percent. At these levels, with a high base rate of national income or even national income per capita, let there be no mistaking that a 1 percent rise in economic development can make a lot of difference.

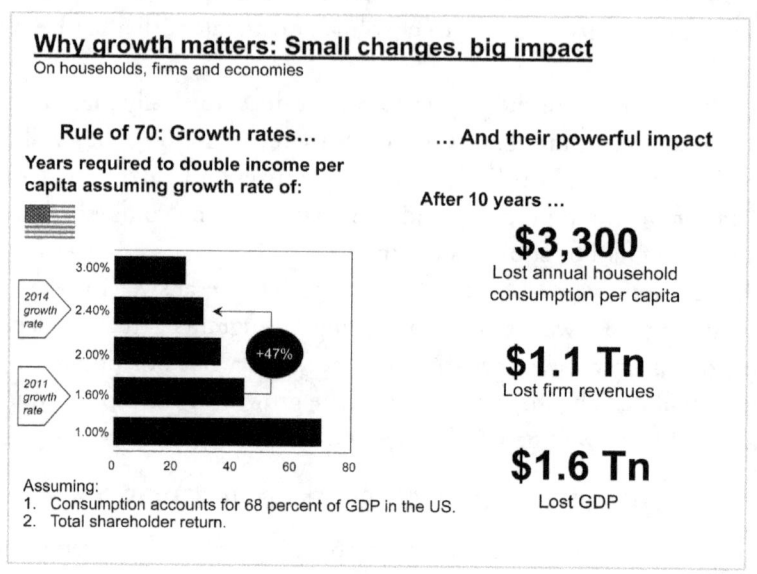

Table generated from BCG Centre for Macroeconomic Analysis (Congressional Budget Office, 2017; Bureau of Economic Analysis, 2017).

To illustrate this: In 2014 the American economy grew by 2.4 percent. At that rate, it would take the United States (US) 30 years to double its income per capita. In 2011, the growth rate was 1.6 percent, just 0.8 percent less. At that rate, they would take 44 years to double its income per capita. That is a 14-year difference. So over 10 years, the difference of less than 1 percent leads to US$3,300 in lost annual consumption per capita for households — more than enough, I think, for that year-end holiday or to pay down student loans. It would translate to US$1.1 trillion in lost revenue for firms, along with the impact on their market valuation, US$1.6 trillion in lost gross domestic product (GDP) that affects growth opportunities and amongst other things, the ability to fund social safety nets.

What if We Cease to Accept Immigrants?

Bringing us back to today and Singapore, I think we know that without immigration, our population and our workforce will be smaller and older. This will have a big impact on economic growth and the long-term dynamism of our economy.

DELIBERATIONS OF THE COMMITTEE ON THE FUTURE ECONOMY

As a member of the Committee on the Future Economy, I can say that we had passionate discussions about the matter of talent that is needed to support the development of the economy of the future, with specific reference to the role of foreign manpower.

Let me share some of the concerns we heard on this topic. We heard about the need and desire to attract talent from across the globe to facilitate the country's digital transformation, to develop sectors like data sciences and cyber security. We heard how small and medium-sized businesses fear for their survival or the business opportunities they are missing out on because they are not able to hire enough workers. One idea was to allow the companies that do want to transform some leeway on hiring foreign workers.

We also heard from foreigners who said that Singapore is the best place to be right now, but who also expressed concerns about talent restrictions that hinder their ability to grow their businesses; as well as unpredictable policy and regulatory changes that hinder their ability to plan. What they would like is for their genuine effort to build the local talent pipeline in their companies to be recognised and rewarded.

Of course, we also appreciate the opposing views to these — worry about competition, the crowding-out of opportunities for Singaporean talent and the challenges of integrating foreigners and the foreign workforce in Singapore. Some even felt that there is a need to avoid corporate welfarism that prevents the weeding-out of inefficient businesses. I think there is agreement however that for the long term, there is the need to move the economy towards higher skills, higher productivity, and to reduce the dependency on foreign labour.

PRODUCTIVITY AND IMMIGRATION

How optimistic can we be with regard to such goals? Let us look back into history. Singapore's challenges in terms of productivity growth are well known but we must realise that a big part of the story is that quite a lot of Singapore's labour input in the years past has been fuelled by immigration. Since 2011, with the tightening of immigration, we have seen a sharp drop in the labour contribution. Initially aimed at reducing low-skilled immigration, more recently we see this tightening reaching into the higher end of the labour market. With that tightening, as well as the drop in capital investment, the outcome seems to be lower GDP growth.

Is there another way? Of course. If we want to cease accepting immigrants and yet want our economy to grow, we can increase birth rates, increase labour force participation to offset the immigrant group. Unfortunately, we have not been able to achieve these in recent years, at least not on a sustainable basis. In that case, we would need more capital to precipitate higher productivity growth which you cannot do without.

Yet, the growth in capital investment has been declining amid the current slowdown, and productivity is growing very slowly across all economies. This global decline in productivity growth actually is a bit of a paradox. We all live in a world of technological progress — but why then has productivity growth gone down, or at least been so slow?

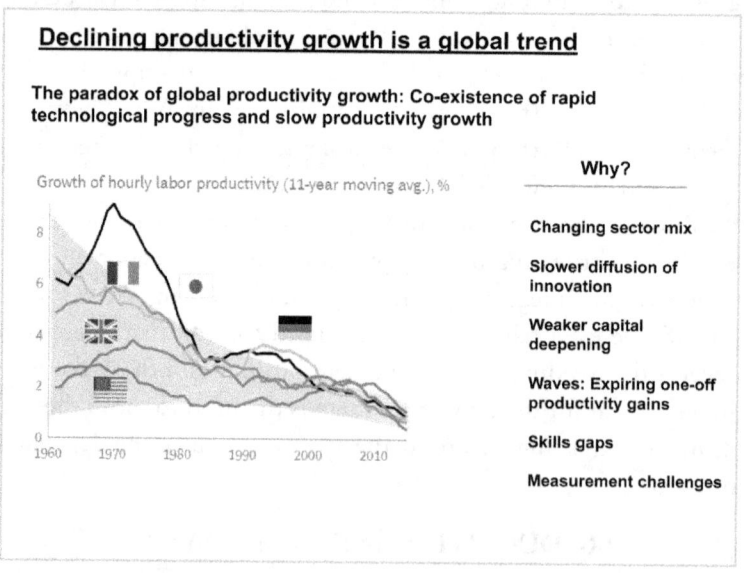

Source: The Conference Board, 2017.

What if We Cease to Accept Immigrants?

Now we looked at the data in the US, and came up with six different explanations for it. They are: the changing sector mix, with more going to less productive sectors; slow diffusion of innovation across firms in the economy; lower capital investment; one-off only productivity gains from previous waves of technology; skills gaps holding back productivity growth in some sectors; and finally, measurement challenges, where we think that perhaps productivity is improving and it is just that we are measuring it incorrectly. Part of this, for example, is because of distorted pricing.

We have not done a similar analysis for Singapore but I think we can imagine that many of the same explanations hold in our case. Of course, we should not extrapolate today's constraints to the future, but the question remains: If we turn off the tap to foreign labour today, where will growth come from?

We can look at Japan as an example. Its economic miracle years are always held up as an indication of how productivity growth can allow for rapid growth without a high immigration ratio. But over the last two decades, even Japan is seeing that they need to start accepting immigrants as their population shrinks and ages rapidly.

So, some have seen the solution to Japan's demographic challenges as a choice between robots on one hand, and immigration on the other. A lot is said about money that is being put into robots, but Japan is also taking steps to open its door to foreign labour, say in the construction sector and domestic services, and now skilled workers can apply for permanent residency after just one year of being in Japan.

In contrast, the US is always thought of as a nation of immigrants, but US immigration has always gone through multiple waves: increased immigration followed by lulls driven by social, political and demographic factors. I think the most interesting thing about the US' experience is the role of the immigrant entrepreneur. This is the crowning achievement of US immigration, at least in my book. If you consider the statistics from a 2013 National Venture Capitalist Association study, between 2006 and 2012, immigrants started 33 percent of US venture-backed companies that went public — a total of 92 such companies. These are companies like Google, Facebook, LinkedIn, Tesla. The value created by these companies is extraordinary: a total market capitalisation (cap) of US$900 billion. Now if these companies were a country, their market cap would rank them 16th in the

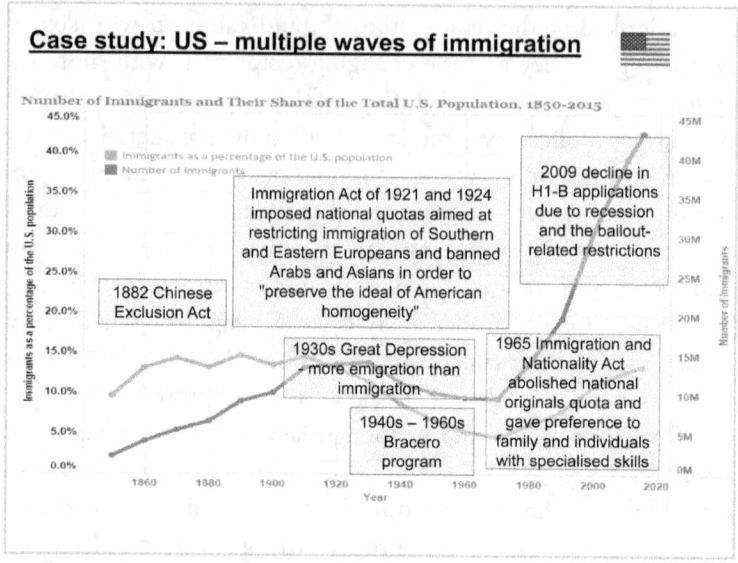

Source: Migration Policy Institute, 2016.

world, higher than Russia, South Africa, Taiwan, and yes, higher than Singapore. These companies employ approximately 600,000 people, the majority of whom are in the US.

As you can see, I think the question of immigration is a tough one. If you pressed me on the question: Can we cease accepting immigrants today? I would say "probably not". Then exactly how many more foreign workers do we need? I think that is a question that will take a lot more data, and alignment on what we, as a country, want our growth rates to be. Unfortunately, that is a question for our politicians and not for me.

IMPLICATIONS

If we believe that the scenarios I shared are plausible and that things can change quickly, the most important thing is for our immigration policy to be adaptive. That would mean reading the change in the signals accurately, course-correcting, driving experimentation and having feedback loops.

For examples of rapid change: On the technology side, look at the evolution of the exponential laws of technology, Moore's Law, Kryder's Law, Butter's Law; look at how AI evolves. Or for changes in economic development, look at what happens to global trade flows and free trade agreements.

What if We Cease to Accept Immigrants?

Signals of change – leading indicators

- Moore's law (computing)
- General AI

- Global trade flows
- EU, ASEAN integration
- TPP, NAFTA, RCEP

- Kryder's law (storage)
- Blockchain based apps

- Gini Coefficient
- Track income of bottom 20% and median income
- Track movement from bottom 20% to top 20%

- Butter's law (bandwidth)
- Cyberthreats

- Domestic political outlook
- Track the Trust Barometer

Finally, the second major implication of what I have set out is that we must not just seek to protect the "Singaporean Core" of workers; we must elevate it. Whether you are in the public sector, you run a business, you are a labour unionist or, you are a citizen or an immigrant, you should try and do this.

Don't just protect the Singaporean core, elevate it

Government	• Drive productivity growth and innovation across the economy • Invest in human capital and help citizens reinvent their careers with education, skills training and modern day apprenticeship • Rethink social systems and policies and foster inclusive culture
Business	• Invest to be at technological frontier • Build local talent pipeline, collaborate with other stakeholders, invest in in-house learning & development • Adopt more inclusive social strategies • Shape a credible, inclusive and trust-inspiring narrative
Unions / Assocs / NGOs	• Step up to help companies and workers prepare and cope through the transition, collaborate with all stakeholders on behalf of workers
Citizens	• Embrace technology in daily lives • Embrace lifelong learning, re-skilling, skills mastery and build resilience and adaptability • Seek help from institutions that can help to raise the relative working conditions and prospects of all workers (government, unions, professional associations) • Be open, kind and gracious
Immigrants	• Embrace Singapore culture and integrate • Be part of the conversation

There is one last point that should be directed to immigrants in Singapore: You can do your part. Integrate and embrace Singapore culture.

From my experience, very few immigrants participate in any kind of public dialogue on immigration, although many of them talk about it in private. In the spirit of national discourse, I think it is time we broaden it so that immigrants can share their stories and aspirations, and I think we will find more commonalities than differences between them and Singaporeans. Hopefully, that will then allow us to talk about immigration with a bit more rationality and empathy on all sides.

REFERENCES

Bureau of Economic Analysis. (2017, September 28). National economic accounts, gross domestic product (GDP), percentage change from preceding period. Retrieved from https://www.bea.gov/national/xls/gdpchg.xls.

Congressional Budget Office. (2017). Budget and economic data. Retrieved from: https://www.cbo.gov/about/products/budget-economic-data#4.

Migration Policy Institute. (2016). U.S. Immigrant population and share over time, 1850-Present. Retrieved from: http://www.migrationpolicy.org/programs/data-hub/charts/immigrant-population-over-time.

The Conference Board. (2017, May). Total Economy Database™ - Data. Retrieved from: https://www.conference-board.org/data/economydatabase/index.cfm?id=27762.

CHAPTER 9

What if the Family is No Longer the Fundamental Building Block of Society?

THANG LENG LENG

It is common for discussions on socio-cultural changes facing Singapore to recognise that the family is changing. The changing family and the repercussions of such changes are certainly challenges not unfamiliar to policymakers in other parts of the world. As the report "The Future of Families to 2030" published by the Organisation for Economic Cooperation and Development (OECD) states — as the family in the OECD area has been undergoing significant transformation since the 1960s, "the extended family has all but disappeared, and the traditional family consisting of a married couple with children has become much less widespread.... The repercussions of these changes on housing, pensions, health and long-term care, labour markets, education and public finances, have been remarkable" (OECD, 2011, p. 7). In Singapore, which has seen gradual changes in the family in recent years, the questions these trends raise are: Will we reach the situation where the family is no longer the fundamental building block of society and, what are the implications of such a scenario?

With the challenges of a rapidly ageing society looming large on the horizon, I would like to consider these questions primarily from the perspective of family support of its older members. What are the perceptions of the family-centric public policy and practices with regard to care of the elderly in Singapore? In the case where the family ceases to be part of the equation of support, what then are the possible substitutes? How do they shape the re-thinking of the family further?

CHANGES IN SINGAPORE FAMILIES

First, let us consider what exactly has changed in Singapore families over the past decades. One obvious indicator is the changing family structure. Family size has declined dramatically as a result of the fall in fertility rate since the country achieved independence. As the national fertility rate dropped from 4.7 in 1965 to 1.24 in 2015, the family has become smaller where having none, one child or two children has become a norm. It is no wonder then that the average household size has shrunk from 4.87 in 1980 to 3.98 in 1994 and 3.39 in 2015 (Department of Statistics (DOS), 2016, p. 117).

A more detailed breakdown of the changes as shown in Table 1 reveals an increase in the percentage of one-generation households (headed by married couples who are childless or not living with children) and one-person households between 2000 and 2014 (Ministry of Social and Family Development (MSF), 2015). Going in the opposite direction, the parent-child nuclear family structure has declined in proportion among all households from 56 to 49 percent; while three-generation households have remained more or less constant at around 10 percent in the same 15-year period (see Table 1).

With rapid population ageing and persistently low fertility rate, we can expect further rise in the percentage of one-person and one-generation households in the future, especially among the older generation who are more

Table 1: Singapore Resident Households by Household Structure, 2000–2014

Household Structure	Number ('000)				Percent			
	2000	2005	2010	2014	2000	2005	2010	2014
Total	915.1	1,024.5	1,145.9	1,200.0	100.0	100.0	100.0	100.0
Nuclear Families	511.0	540.2	565.2	591.6	55.8	52.7	49.3	49.3
Married without Co-residing Children	96.9	120.7	140.0	173.0	10.6	11.8	12.2	14.4
3G Households	89.6	101.9	121.9	113.9	9.8	9.9	10.6	9.5
Single Parents with Children	63.1	65.7	78.2	81.7	6.9	6.4	6.8	6.8
One-Person	75.4	103.3	139.9	134.8	8.2	10.1	12.2	11.2
Other households	79.1	92.7	100.8	105.0	8.6	9.1	8.8	8.8

Source: MSF, 2015a, p. 18.

likely to live on their own due to their preference for independent living, or because their children have become independent, they never had children, they stayed single and for other reasons. Such changes in family structure have implications on intergenerational support and care provision especially with regard to the elderly.

Another harbinger of the transformation of the family in Singapore is the widely perceived changing values of the young towards the concept. Besides pointing to the emergence of values such as "individualism" which has contributed to a lower desire among the younger generation to have children, the older generation often laments the decline in the value of filial piety upon which, in the Singapore context, much of the traditional intergenerational family support is based. Specifically, people in the 50s belonging to the sandwich generation where they have to care for their ageing parents and young children, often regard themselves as the last generation of filial children who still have the sense of responsibility of caring for their seniors. However, they do not expect the same from their children in the future.

The third way in which we see change in the notion of the family is in the emergence of its diverse forms. Although "the family" usually refers to a legally married heterosexual couple with children born within that legal union, the OECD report reminds us that this traditional form has become less widespread. In reality, the modern family now comes with greater diversity.

Public policy in Singapore generally defines "the family" in its traditional form which may disadvantage families that do not have such a configuration. Fortunately, over the years, we have seen changes in the legal arrangements covering public housing, income tax deductions, Central Provident Fund (CPF), healthcare and so on that suggest an increasing effort by the government to address the needs of family types that divert from that "traditional" form (MSF, 2015b). In fact, family diversity arising from divorce, separation, widowhood, birth out of wedlock, singlehood, alternate and multi-generational arrangements and so on is already part and parcel of what constitutes the modern family here, but there is still room to improve the process of policymaking so that the needs of the diverse modern family unit is taken into consideration.

THE SUPPORT OF OLDER MEMBERS IN SINGAPORE FAMILIES

One significant implication of the changing family in an ageing society context like ours is the concern about who older persons can turn to in time of need.

Singapore's ageing policy is known for its family-centric focus. As the "Report on the Ageing Population" put out by the government-convened Committee on Ageing Issues (CAI) in 2006 states, "We believe that the family is the primary care-giving unit and the bedrock of support for seniors. The family must be supported and strengthened in its ability to care for its older members to ensure that institutionalisation remains a measure of last resort" (CAI, 2006, p. 12). The policy orientation reinforces the "Many Helping Hands" approach to social support — where the individual should bear the first level of responsibility for his well-being, failing which, the hierarchy of responsibility will move to the family, then to support from voluntary welfare organisations (VWOs) and lastly, the state. The Maintenance of Parents Act (MPA) of 1995, which was introduced to enable indigent older people to seek legal recourse for financial support from their children, is often perceived as entrenching the value of filial piety and the state's overt expectation that the family be the first line of care after the individual himself.

The family focus in ageing policy, which has stayed consistent since the first national report on ageing policy in 1984 and the accompanying precepts of filial piety have received criticism from scholars and others.[1] For example, the state is criticised for doing less in care provision than other governments (see Rozario & Rosetti, 2012), and that its emphasis on familism gives family members little choice because it reinforces the notion that family care is the best form of care for frail older persons. Even if this is so, in reality, family members who are expected to be caregivers may not be the most suitable and qualified to provide that care (Teo *et al.*, 2006).

However, such criticism should not be simply taken as an objection to the idea that the family should provide care, but more of a reflection of fatigue towards the overtly explicit message that family *must* care. In fact, it is normal

---

[1] The first national report on ageing policies in Singapore of 1989 is widely known as the Howe Report named after then Minister for Health, Howe Yoon Cheong who chaired the first committee to study the problems of the aged in 1982.

for a government to expect that the family will provide for its older members, except that in most countries, the role of the family is often assumed and implied, rather than overtly and constantly stated or even legally enforced such as through the MPA.

Paradoxically, the government's repeated emphasis on the family in ageing care provision may suggest that there is the uncertainty ahead about whether we can truly continue to rely on the family as the first line of support after the individual himself. In the "Report on the Ageing Population", while we find a reiteration of the importance placed on the role of the family for caregiving, the challenges facing the family is also recognised: "[G]iven the trend of smaller families and the increasing number of singles, the CAI notes that the role of the family as the first line of care will be increasingly challenged. We will need to find ways to strengthen and help families to fulfil their roles" (CAI, 2006, p. 12).

Others may perceive the government's relentless effort to ensure the family takes responsibility for their older members as a *kiasu* attitude; a way to ensure that all risk is avoided or mitigated. After all, Singaporeans have reaffirmed through various survey responses that they value the family, they are committed to the institution of family, and have strong filial values towards their parents.[2] This unconditional love for parents is even affirmed by a majority of the millennials (below 30 years old) who are seen as the group most likely to abandon so-called "traditional" values like filial piety (Mathews, 2015). While such responses are encouraging, a gap is sometimes observed between what people perceive or what they desire on the one hand, and the reality on the other. For instance, while people show the desire for a strong family relationship, in reality, they may be spending very little time with the family because of their long hours at work (Channel NewsAsia (CNA), 2015).

How about the older persons' perceptions of receiving support from the family? Recent studies have shown that more people desire independence from the family. However, this does not rule out an ambivalent attitude among some. In a study on the lay perceptions of successful ageing, at least half of the 50 to 69-year-olds surveyed in the study ($n = 1,540$) simultaneously highlighted independence from family and dependence on

---

[2] See for example, "Survey on Social Attitudes of Singaporeans" (MSF, various years from 2003 to 2013).

the family (in terms of care by children) as constituting successful ageing (Feng & Straughan, 2017).

In another survey on Singaporeans' aspirations for aged care ($n = 998$), 84 percent in the 60 to 75 age group expressed their desire to live independently from their children. Respondents in this age group also expressed the willingness to live in alternative housing and care arrangements, such as senior's apartments (66 percent), nursing homes (58 percent) and retirement villages (48 percent). Although the expectation of living with or close to children ranked lower than the categories of living arrangements mentioned above, there remained a substantial number — 33 percent — who said they would be willing to live near their children, and 46 percent who would be willing to live with their children. Among the younger respondents in the 30 to 44 age group, those indicating their preference to live in a retirement village was particularly high — 66 percent. In comparison, among this younger age group 27 percent said they were willing to live with their children in the future but more, 45 percent said they would be willing to live near their children (Lien Foundation and NTUC Income, 2016).

These findings indicate a decreasing desire to rely on the family in old age. This is corroborated by findings of qualitative studies too where older respondents have expressed uncertainty about being able to rely on support from their children. Reasons for the ambivalence range from their perception of the changing values among the young, the strategy of expecting the worst to avoid disappointment, and their desire to avoid becoming a burden to their children (Thang & Mehta, forthcoming).

With the emerging norm towards independent living among the older generation, coupled with changes in the family and competing demands faced by the younger generation, it is inevitable that both the old and young generations will become more reserved in their expectation on the family to serve as a pillar of support in old age. When this happens, if there is no concerted policy effort to strengthen and support the family in its role to provide care and support, we can expect a gradual disintegration of the family as the bedrock of support.

ALTERNATIVES IN INSTRUMENTAL AND EMOTIONAL SUPPORT

Although the government still actively adopts a family-focused policy in old age support, we have witnessed in the past decade or so, that there have been efforts made to enable older persons to live independently too. This includes measures such as the studio apartment scheme, the reverse mortgage scheme and CPF annuity scheme to boost the size of one's nest egg upon retirement; improvements in insurance and various forms of financial support for greater healthcare affordability; and the building of more nursing homes to meet the long-term care needs of the frail elderly population. There is no doubt that the ramping up of such policy measures and schemes is significant especially in ensuring adequate financial and healthcare support in later life, but how can social and emotional support be adequately met if one can no longer rely on the family?

If successful ageing is a process of adaptation through selection, optimisation and compensation strategies (Baltes & Baltes, 1990), there are some alternative forms of support that we can explore to deal with the shortfall in family support.

Friends and neighbours

It comes with little surprise that friendship plays an important role in one's well-being. Having emotionally close friends can strengthen one's social support and serve to compensate for the limits of the family in providing the support (Lang & Carstensen, 1994). In studies, older persons who are less connected with the family have often identified close friends as the primary core of support. These friends not only provide companionship to address social and emotional needs but they also are a source of financial and instrumental support (Thang, 2015).

Compared to having such friends, neighbours seem quite an unlikely but nonetheless important source of strong support for many in Singapore. Even if it is not of the same quality of neighbourly help and community ties as the old *kampung* (village) days, the HDB Sample Household Survey (2013) found neighbourly ties to be present largely in the form of exchange of greetings and casual conversations. A study of community ties and help patterns among the low-income rental flats residents found quite a strong presence of informal mutual help among the residents, especially when they are long-term residents in the same block of flats (Leng, 2016). For older persons living alone, such active neighbourly exchanges may surpass their family and friends in playing a significant role in support of one's well-being. As a qualitative study revealed, neighbours not only serve as companions, but also provide essential practical help such as offering cooked meals to one another, assistance in shopping for groceries, and looking out for one another's well-being (Thang, 2015). As the Chinese saying goes, "Relatives far away cannot be compared with neighbours close by", so examples of neighbourly bonding in rental flats offer insights into the potential of community mutual support networks in compensating for distant family help (if any), and reinforces the need to design and build neighbourhood environments that are conducive to community living and social interaction.

Pets

Pets are known to provide intangible yet valuable support to older persons, especially among those living alone or in group living, and have been studied for their positive impact on the health of older persons (Dembicki & Anderson, 1996). Owning a pet not only helps in contributing to better health of the owners, but could also aid in expanding their social circle with fellow pet owners they meet on walks with their pets. They also allow older persons to feel a sense of purpose as they care for their pets. When pet owners build intimate relationships with their pets, many would regard their pets as family and some people have even included their pets in wills to receive an inheritance when they pass on.

In Singapore, pet ownership among older persons is little studied but it has the likelihood of becoming more popular as the number of older persons living in single or one generation households rises in the future. How will the definition of family be expanded if pets are increasingly accepted as a substitute for family members in elderly-only households?

Robots

In the face of the likely shortage of caregivers for older persons in a rapidly ageing population, countries like Japan have been active in developing robots to provide nursing care and help perform daily tasks to assist older persons at home and in institutional settings. More recently, besides "work" robots, new therapeutic robots such as Paro and Pepper, which are able to display emotions, have caught public attention for their apparent ability to bond with humans and perhaps stand in place of the family. In Singapore, robots that can engage in conversation with humans have been developed. In China, "intelligent nursing robots" that can monitor the taking of medication and blood pressure are being developed for deployment across the country. However, a pilot programme at a nursing home in China found that although robots performed a functional role in meeting nursing needs, residents nonetheless perceived them more as companions who can dance and sing and therefore can be used to replace the presence of family members. As one resident who used to expect her children and grandchildren's visit said, "Before, I had expected that they might come to see me.... But since I have robots, it is fine that they rarely visit me" (Connor & Wei, 2016).

Scholars like Sherry Turkle caution against the phenomenon of "outsourcing" to machines tasks such as understanding and caring for each other which she feels is best carried out by humans (Turkle, 2012; 2014). She argues that compensating for the lack of family with robots reflects "poorly on us and how we think about older people when they try to tell us the stories of their lives" (Turkle, 2014). However, if the family no longer has the capacity to make time for its older members, there may be little choice for the lonely older persons.

MOVING FORWARD: THE FAMILY+ FRAMEWORK

Today, Singapore is situated at a tension point where the family which is already changing is nonetheless expected to face the stress of coping with the rapidly ageing population. The limits of the family could lead to the move away from the ideology of the family as the fundamental primary unit of care and support in society. In the case where such a trend seems inevitable, policies and practices of welfare systems in Western countries, especially the Nordic countries, will serve as ready examples for policymakers as they consider how to shape their policies for the care of the elderly here.

The challenge, though, is how to move forward with a continuing focus on family as a primary source of support in the circumstances of the changing family and demographic ageing? As the changing values on filial piety among the younger generation is one source of concern affecting family support of the old, sociologist Tan Ern Ser (2015) has proposed that love, instead of filial piety, should be regarded as a more reliable basis for the support of parents because it is relationship-centric, and not self-centric. Only when one is motivated to support one's parents out of love for them, and not because of moral obligation or the law, will there be a sustainable basis for that care.

However, Tan has observed that it is those who are in the higher income group who have a higher tendency to say that "love for one's parents" is the basis for providing financially for dependent parents. Yet, even if "love" were to prevail over filial piety in ensuring the support of their older parents, the family could still be limited in its capacity to do so. Hence, along with the emphasis on the value of love, I would like to suggest a family$^+$ framework which recognises that the family has its limits and will need to be supported through a comprehensive array of social policy and a broader network of significant others. Here the + (plus) will serve to assist the individuals and families in their capacity to support their loved ones. Although one could argue that the government has already been ramping up efforts to support older individuals such as through the provision of various financing and healthcare schemes mentioned earlier, the idea of family$^+$ is a call for a more inclusive approach so that emerging diverse forms of family can also be tapped to provide that support. Think, for instance, of extending the context of family to include nieces and nephews. A family$^+$ approach that emphasises the nurturing and strengthening of the family in its diverse forms across all policy arenas will hopefully be able to keep the worries of the disintegration of the family as we currently know it, at bay.

REFERENCES

Baltes, P. B., & Baltes, M. M. (1990). Psychological perspectives on successful aging: The model of selective optimization with compensation. In Baltes P. B., & Baltes, M. M. (Eds.), *Successful aging: Perspectives from the behavioral sciences*. New York: Cambridge University Press.

Channel NewsAsia. (2015, May 26). Singaporeans value families: Survey. Retrieved from: http://www.channelnewsasia.com/news/singapore/singaporeans-value/1872958.html.

Committee on Ageing Issues. (2006). Report on the ageing population. Retrieved from: https://www.moh.gov.sg/content/dam/moh_web/Publications/Reports/2006/3/Chapter%202%20-20Focus%20on%20Ageing%20Issues.pdf.

Connor, N., & Wei, C. (2016, November 26). Together in electric dreams: Robots replace family love for China's lonely elderly. *The Telegraph*. Retrieved from: http://www.telegraph.co.uk/news/2016/11/26/together-electric-dreams-robots-replace-family-love-chinas-lonely/.

Dembicki, D., & Anderson, J. (1996). Pet ownership may be a factor in improved health of the elderly. *Journal of Nutrition for the Elderly*, 15(3): 15–31.

Department of Statistics Singapore (DOS). (2016). Population trends 2016. Retrieved from: http://www.singstat.gov.sg/docs/default-source/default-document-library/publications/publications_and_papers/population_and_population_structure/population2016.pdf.

Feng, Q., Staughan, P. T. (2017). What does successful aging mean? Lay perception of successful aging among elderly Singaporeans. *Journal of Gerontology B Psychological Science and Social Sciences, 72*(2): 204–213. doi: 10.1093/geronb/gbw151.

Housing and Development Board (HDB). (2014). Public housing in Singapore: Social well-being of HDB communities. HDB sample household survey 2013. Retrieved from: www.hdb.gov.sg/cs/infoweb/monograph-2-29-dec-2014.

Lang, F. R., & Carstensen, L. L. (1994). Close emotional relationships in late life: Further support for proactive aging in the social domain. *Psychology and Aging, 9*(2), 315.

Leng, T. H. (2016). *Community bonding among public rental flat dwellers*. Project dissertation. Real Estate Department, National University of Singapore.

Lien Foundation and NTUC Income. (2016, October 18). Survey reveals Singaporeans' concerns and aspirations of aged care. Media release. Retrieved from: https://income.com.sg/about-us/press-releases/survey-reveals-singaporeans-concerns-and-aspirations.

Mathews, M. (2015, June 1). The changing Singapore family. *The Straits Times*. Retrieved from: http://www.straitstimes.com/opinion/the-changing-singapore-family.

Ministry of Social and Family Development (MSF). (2015a). Families and households in Singapore, 2000–2014. *Statistics Series Paper No. 2/2015*. Singapore: MSF. Retrieved from: https://app-stg.msf.gov.sg/Portals/0/Summary/publication/FDG/Statistics%20Series%20-%20Families%20and%20Households%20in%20Singapore.pdf.

Ministry of Social and Family Development (MSF). (2015b, May 22). Social service partners discuss emerging family trends and support to strengthen families. Press release. Retrieved from: https://www.msf.gov.sg/media-room/Pages/Social-Service-Partners-Discuss-Emerging-Family-Trends-and-Support-to-Strengthen-Families.aspx.

Teo, P., Mehta, K., Thang, L. L., & Chan, A. (2006). *Ageing in Singapore: Service needs and the state.* London: Routledge.

Organisation for Economic Cooperation and Development (OECD). (2011). *The futures of families to 2030: Projections, policy challenges and policy options — A synthesis report.* Retrieved from: www.oecd.org/futures/49093502.pdf.

Rozario, P., & Rosetti, A. (2012). Many helping hands: A review and analysis of long-term care policies, programs, and practices in Singapore. *Journal of Gerontological Social Work*, 55(7), 641–658.

Tan, E. S. (2015, July). Class and social orientations: Key findings from the social stratification survey 2011. *IPS Exchange Number 4*. Institute of Policy Studies.

Thang, L. L. (2015). Social networks and the wellbeing of older adults in Singapore. In Cheng, S., Chi, I., Li, L. W., Woo J., & Fung, H. H. (Eds.), *Successful aging: Asian perspectives.* Springer.

Thang, L. L., & Metha, K. (2017). Intergenerational relations, ageing and family in Singapore. In Koh, B. S. (Ed.), *The State of Aging in Singapore.* Singapore: Tsao Foundation Longevity Press. Forthcoming.

Turkle, S. (2012). *Alone together: Why we expect more from technology and less from each other.* New York: Basic Books.

Turkle, S. (2014, July 25). How ... are ... you ... feeling ... today? When a robot is a caregiver. *The New York Times.* Retrieved from https://www.nytimes.com/2014/07/26/opinion/when-a-robot-is-a-caregiver.html?_r=1.

SECTION **IV**

Looking Ahead

CHAPTER 10

What if Singapore Becomes a Two- or Multi-Party System?

ONG YE KUNG

"What if Singapore becomes a two- or multi-party system?"

I could make this a boring discussion by insisting that we are already a multi-party system since many parties participate in our general elections, but that would be a cop out.

Instead, let us train our attention on the elephant in the room — which is the People's Action Party (PAP). The scenario painted for us is that by 2065, it is replaced by several smaller elephants — political parties — that will take turns to govern after each election or rule through coalitions.

This will be a drastic departure from the status quo which we cannot rule out half a century from now. The question is: What happens then?

I would like to present my thoughts in three parts. First, while life will change in many ways, we will adapt and in many ways, life will go on. Second, I will explain why this can give rise to a couple of serious long-term risks for Singapore. Third, I will address the question that many Singaporeans will also ask: "What is the PAP going to do about it?"

LIFE GOES ON

First, what will change and yet, how will life go on?

A major change that will stem from becoming a multi-party system will be the shifting of the political ground. Expect intense jostling — different parties reaching out to various groups to garner support. The trade union movement may not be as cohesive as it is today where it works with the PAP in a symbiotic relationship. It may be split into two or more groupings, or there may be a competing federation, like in 1961 when the existing Singapore Trades Union Congress split into the Singapore Association of Trade Unions and the National Trades Union Congress. Likewise, there will be split affiliations amongst associations, clans, societies, recreational clubs, civil society organisations, socio-political sites, sports and arts bodies, and so on. Media houses may split too.

It is not a new phenomenon. We have seen this happen in more hotly contested constituencies. After the general election in 2011 when the Workers' Party (WP) won Aljunied Group Representation Constituency (GRC), I found myself becoming the opposition politician in that GRC. There were groups that would invite me as guest-of-honour to their events, and others that would invite the WP members of parliament. Most would invite both, and I got the feeling that the guests enjoyed watching the jostling. In a multi-party system, the scale of that happening will likely be larger, nationwide, at events, and behind the scenes.

I believe the institution that is most likely to be tested is the civil service. The holy grail of the civil service is to be politically neutral and serve whichever party forms the government regardless of how different the incoming party may be from the outgoing one in governance philosophy. Public service officers must lay out the policy options, state the pros and cons, let the political leaders with the mandate decide, and then, they must support the decision. It is a professional ideal, but in practice, it is easier said than done. You can work on one set of policies for five years and someone new can come along to ask you to undo everything you have done and move in a new direction. We see that happening now — the Affordable Healthcare Act in the United States (US) is being unwound, the country has also withdrawn from the Trans-Pacific Partnership. That can be very frustrating and disheartening to public service leaders.

It is useful to see how other countries deal with it. America ended up politicising the higher echelons of its civil service. The top few layers of bureaucrats are political appointees, and whenever there is a change in who is the president, they are all replaced. That is why the new Trump administration has to make 4,000 appointments.

The alternative is the Australian or the British system, where all civil servants in the ministries stay intact, but a minister's office is packed with his own staffers — presumably more aligned to his thinking. In Australia, ministers spend most of their time with these staffers in parliament, and not the civil servants in the ministries — because parliament is where the political contest is.

We will have to adapt to all these if the scenario comes to pass, which also means that the status quo as we know it will change. But adapt we will.

THE MAJOR RISKS

Second, I will touch on the real long-term risks for Singapore of a multi-party system that are beyond adapting and getting used to. The risk is not so much a result of being in a multi-party system per se, but the forces and processes that will lead us there.

For a two- or multi-party system to take shape, there must first have been at least two paths, sufficiently different, for our country to take. These paths can be a narrow fork in the road that can even merge further down, or a T-junction pointing in opposite directions and will never meet.

Take the United Kingdom (UK) for example. From the mid-1990s to early 2010s, the Conservatives and New Labour both believed in a pro-business, market economy that upholds equality of opportunities instead of equality in outcomes. Both eschewed labour unrest and strikes — which was a major shift for New Labour. The key divergence in policy was probably in their attitudes towards the European Union (EU). Today, that has widened into a gulf between those who believe in the idea of the UK leaving the EU or "Brexit" in one camp and that of remaining in the EU, in the other camp. That difference has split British society between the young and old, urban and rural residents, the more and the less educated.

In the US, the key historical divergence between the Republicans and Democrats was slavery. The situation has evolved. Slavery is no more, and today, the two parties hold distinct views on the size of government, taxation, abortion and gun control. In the 2016 presidential election, those positions widened, pitting nationalism against globalisation, whites versus people of other races. Both presidential candidates have openly acknowledged that it was a bitter and divisive election.

Political parties are essential in representing the diverse views of people, and elections, a necessary and relatively peaceful process by which to find compromises in policy positions to seek a way forward for the country. This is the essence of democracy. Yet, that same defining quality can take a nasty twist, sow discord and divide societies. Hence Winston Churchill said, "… democracy is the worst form of Government except all those other forms that have been tried from time to time."

Fifty years from now, if we have a multi-party system, what will define the key political differences between political parties? Where will that partisan line emerge? Would it be over the extent to which we should subsidise public services, healthcare and social assistance? If that is so, it may well be something we can manage. What if it is over something more sinister that divides Singapore by race, language or religion? As we all know, politics, race and religion is a toxic mix. If that happens, we will be broken as a country and society.

Another major risk is whether a multi-party system will slow down decision-making and our nimbleness in navigating an ever-changing external environment. If we had a multi-party system back in 1965, would we have become a developed economy and country so quickly?

Back then, in that post-colonial era, we could move to attract foreign direct investment from multinational corporations when it was not politically correct to do so. We forged omni-directional, bilateral free trade agreements while others pledged allegiance to the World Trade Organization's multilateral system. We must move fast in embracing new digital technologies, even though it can be uncomfortable and disruptive.

If we envisage a future of tough challenges — a shifting geopolitical landscape, more intense economic competition, worrying demographic trends, rising sea levels — unity, common purpose and the ability to move faster than others will be central and vital for us. While other countries are either slow but big, or small but fast, will we end up suffering the worst of both worlds — small and slow?

The current system has worked well for the majority of Singaporeans so far. It still gets my vote as the best system for Singapore.

HERE'S WHAT WE NEED TO DO

So, given these risks, what can the PAP do about them?

To answer this question, let me rewind to 2011 when I was first introduced as a PAP candidate. I was asked by a journalist what I thought of a single-party system in Singapore. I said that our equilibrium as a small

What if Singapore Becomes a Two- or Multi-Party System?

country may well be single-party rule. That party can be the PAP today, but some other party in the future — so long it is the most capable at that time.

You know that between Singaporeans living in Changi and Jurong, their concerns and views on national issues may be somewhat different, but nothing compared to the great differences you are likely to find between people living in Alaska and New York City, Jakarta and the eastern- and western-most places in the Indonesian archipelago. For big countries, geographical separation translates into different lifestyles, outlook, values and political affinities, which then lends itself to multi-party politics.

The one-party dominant system in the case of Singapore, is not a prescription, but the most likely outcome of choice — a result of free and fair elections. It is no different from Massachusetts being dominated by Democrats for long periods, or Scotland dominated by Labour previously, and now, the Scottish National Party. Smallness and concentration do often come together.

So the answer to the question of what the PAP is going to do about it is that we must make sure the current system continues to work for all Singaporeans!

To do so, we must understand what factors made it work so far. Complacency, elitism and corruption are not inevitable outcomes of one-party dominant rule alone. After all, these ills have shown up across all political systems.

The PAP knows that our integrity must be unquestionable. If something goes wrong, it will be rectified and the perpetrators must face the consequences; that action has to be swift.

The PAP must be a party that is open-minded. It has to keep up with the changing expectations of the population — so that we can be at the forefront of new ideas, with policies that are adapted to the changing needs of society and our people. We must never think that today's solutions are the best there are. We have to keep our eyes and ears open to changes in our surroundings, consult widely, improve our co-creation skills, and work together with citizens in finding solutions to unfolding issues. The PAP must attract talent from as diverse a background as possible to serve the country. That is why at the end of every parliamentary term, the PAP replaces a quarter to a third of the people we place on our electoral slates compared to the previous one.

The PAP must constantly reflect on its performance especially in areas that it has not done well, and even on why the Singapore Dream may not have worked out so well for some Singaporeans. Our policies must be rooted in the ground; a sizeable proportion of our work must be on the ground. In this age of inequality, ours cannot just be a system which rewards only the best and brightest. It must also be a system that compensates for poor family circumstances and the role of luck.

CONCLUSION

Every country in the world is different. A country's success is idiosyncratic and can never be replicated wholesale by another. The formula for success is based on different political processes. Singapore's formula may well be a single-party system.

Ultimately, the political future of a country will be determined by the will of its people. If the people wish for a change to a multi-party system, it will be so. The job of the opposition parties is to highlight to people the risks of the current system. Likewise, it is the job of the PAP today to do our best to make sure that Singapore flourishes, point out the risks of a multi-party system for a small country like ours and keep out the ills of complacency, elitism and corruption.

Whatever the "what ifs" — single- or multi-party system — among all parties and all Singaporeans, we need singularity of purpose and a wide agreement on the means of implementing this purpose. This is not mere politics, but it is about our collective journey, as a people, as a country, to improve the lives of all.

CHAPTER 11

The Real Question Behind "What if Singapore Becomes a Two- or Multi-Party System?"

HO KWON PING

THE REAL QUESTION: WHAT IF THE PAP'S POLITICAL DOMINANCE IS BROKEN

After Donald Trump's almost surreal inauguration on January 20, 2017, the Institute of Policy Studies' (IPS) conference entitled "What If" appears not just prescient in hindsight, but is an urgently needed exercise in future-think. The unthinkable can become the improbable, then the quite possible and sometimes, even reality in an increasingly uncertain world.

So, what is the unthinkable, improbable, what-if political scenario for Singapore?

Here, IPS is being coy with its disingenuously bland topic: "What if Singapore becomes a two- or multi-party system?" After all, unless IPS believes Singapore is like Cuba or North Korea, it is quite obvious that we are *already* a multi-party system to the extent that multiple parties freely and openly contend in general elections. However, as a *one-party dominant* system, we do not have a *pendulum* democracy where a dynamic political equilibrium is sustained over the long term through political power alternating between two dominant parties providing checks and balances against each other.

IPS' real question is what in my recent book *The Ocean in a Drop* I called the elephant-in-the-room issue: What if one-party dominance is broken, the People's Action Party (PAP) loses in a general election and another political party forms the government?

The PAP itself considered this possibility long ago. Many will recall that the pioneer PAP prime minister, the late Mr Lee Kuan Yew, foresaw that scenario of a "freak election" where an electorate may (in his view) unintentionally and irresponsibly vote out the PAP. His solution was to create the Elected Presidency as a check against what he considered a "rogue government".

What if, however, a freak election is not a freak event but instead becomes institutionalised and Singapore does become a pendulum democracy? Would it be good, bad, or neutral for Singaporeans? How likely is it?

A traditional liberal would welcome this prospect as a sign of progress towards full participatory democracy. After all, one of the touchstones of Western liberal democracy is the concept of a two-party pendulum democracy as the bulwark of long-term, sustainable governance. After Brexit, Donald Trump and other recent or upcoming elections in Europe, we know that faith in traditional Western liberal democracy has been shaken enough for it to no longer be the yardstick by which political maturity or sustainability is measured. This is especially among those who are alarmed by the populist, nationalist sentiments that seemed to have carried the ground in the Brexit Referendum and American election; one where the narrative was to exclude or marginalise minorities and foreigners, and stoke ambivalence against globalisation. It seemed like democracy had turned in on itself with those illiberal choices.

A more universal and comprehensive yardstick is the quality of the social contract between a political leadership and its body politic regardless of whether the formal political structure is a two-party pendulum democracy, a monopolistic Communist regime, or a single-party dominant system. The depth of that social contract and by implication, the political legitimacy of the ruling elite, depends on a complex and yet subtle blend of factors for which successive Chinese dynasties coined the euphemism, "the mandate of heaven".

Should that mandate ever erode beyond repair, no amount of two-party or multi-party democracy can save a political regime or ruling dynasty. Traditional pendulum politics does not by itself guarantee genuine participatory democracy: the present crisis of liberal democracy and lurch towards extremism and populism in the United States and Europe, as mentioned above, is eloquent testimony to this depressing reality.

THE REAL CONCERN BEHIND ANTICIPATING POLITICAL CHANGE IN SINGAPORE

Against this backdrop then, the critical question facing Singapore in 2065 is not simply whether an accidental freak election or a sustainable pendulum democracy should or might occur. It is about whether the social contract between elite governance and the body politic can become so strained and frayed that a crisis of political legitimacy may thrust unexpected, extremist scenarios ranging from rule by a military-dominated junta to unstable coalition governments, into reality.

In other words, what might happen to get us from where we are today, a bastion of political stability, to the uncertainties now plaguing the rest of the world? Let me ask and then answer three further questions in pursuit of this issue.

First, what events could lead to a massive loss of legitimacy or confidence in the PAP or the current political system?

Second, what are the chances of these events happening?

Third, is a two-party pendulum democracy a likely, stable and sustainable option? Alternatively, what might realistically evolve in the specific Singapore context?

Let me address the first question in a circumspect manner, by alluding to other Asian democracies. The closest though imperfect parallels are India and Taiwan. In both countries, the founding party of the nation — the Indian Congress party and the Kuomintang (KMT) — were led by charismatic leaders, Jawaharlal Nehru and Chiang Kai Shek, respectively. They were worlds apart both in personality as well as in their party structures but possessed as founding fathers, an unquestioned legitimacy. After their passing, their offspring — Indira Gandhi and Chiang Ching Kuo — succeeded them (albeit with brief interludes in India) but after them, both the party leadership and parties themselves started to decline.

Three identical things happened in both parties:

First, nepotism prevented the rise of younger, meritocratic elites vying within the party for ascendancy, resulting in sycophants all clustering around the dynastic heirs like in some archaic monarchy.

Second, the values, policies and solutions which led the founding party to success became sacrosanct; sacred cows that could not be questioned even if their relevance started to wane. A sense of political complacency settled like fine dust over even the internal insurgents and overcame any impetus towards change.

Third, a culture of entitlement led to endemic corruption, both political and financial, the final blow in an inexorable decline of legitimacy.

Should that fate, which has befallen almost all founding parties in electoral democracies over time affect the PAP in coming decades, we have the scenario for disruptive change.

The second question is: how likely is this to happen?

The short answer is: not very likely in the next quarter-century, or around 20 to 25 years. Beyond that, no one knows.

Why 20 years — perhaps too optimistic for some and too pessimistic for others? I chose this time span because I assume that under our present system, even when the present prime minister, Mr Lee Hsien Loong retires, he will assume the mantle of senior minister or minister mentor, and his cohort of leaders will remain like tribal elders — there to guide successive leadership teams not so much in policymaking but in the preservation of political values, self-discipline and vision which congeal into a lasting political culture.

History has shown that the values of a founding political culture can usually be transmitted with vigour down three to four generations. Beyond that, complacency and entitlement usually overwhelm the messianic urgency and self-discipline found in pioneer values. One can only hope that future PAP leaders after our current leadership have long passed from the scene, can learn from history.

They will have a few advantages, not least being a young nation, a new political culture of anti-corruption, meritocracy and multiculturalism did not have to battle the centuries of deep divisions which afflicted say, Indian civilisation. As Sri Lanka's civil war has shown, a relatively short period of self-serving political opportunism and populism can spiral out of control rapidly. So who is to say, from what we have already seen with the descent into opportunism in even mature, developed European and American societies, that our future leaders will be so self-disciplined as to eschew even a shred of self-interest, especially if their popularity starts to wane?

The Real Question Behind "What if Singapore Becomes a Two- or Multi-Party System?"

As for nepotism, there are no current signs of this happening with a Lee dynasty clinging to power or promoting only its relatives. Anti-corruption has now become not just government policy but a fundamental value of our people. The government has shown signs that even sacred cow policies can be re-examined if they are no longer relevant. We witnessed the PAP government accept the need to tighten up the economy's reliance on cheaper foreign manpower in 2010; reverse its stance on ministerial salaries and slash them by more than a third in 2012; reduce the over-emphasis on academic credentials with the calibration of how the high-stakes Primary School Leaving Examinations are graded as announced in 2013; and then, place more emphasis on skills-training, competencies, performance and therefore give recognition to a "continuous meritocracy" in hiring and rewarding workers, starting with changes in public service personnel policies, announced in 2014. We can think of more.

For those reasons, I remain, using that clichéd phrase, cautiously optimistic. We know however that to some extent, that is whistling in the dark.

When I was a student in Taiwan in the late 1960s, no one could have imagined the decline of the KMT and its future electoral loss, or the rise of a seemingly radical party like the Democratic Progressive Party. It all happened in a few decades. It can happen here too.

The third and possibly most intriguing question is whether the scenario leading towards pendulum democracy in Singapore is the most desirable and likely long-term outcome? And if not, what are the alternatives?

Here we have a conundrum. History has generally shown, despite recent events in the West, that a pendulum democracy offers a more sustainable, dynamic equilibrium than a single-party dominant system which has no competition and falls into complacent entitlement.

On the other hand, to move from the generally well-governed stability of our current single-party dominant system to a pendulum democracy implies that a massive loss of legitimacy by the ruling party has to first occur. That is not necessarily desirable, and of course, not even likely given the current robustness of the PAP and the weakness of the opposition parties.

DODGING POLITICAL OSSIFICATION AND A FRAYING SOCIAL COMPACT — TWO SUGGESTIONS

The danger of a single-party dominant system is political ossification over time, as the sense of entitlement encourages the nepotism, complacency and corruption which inevitably led to the demise — and eventual re-emergence of course — of even the most idealistic founding parties, some of which I have mentioned above.

Therefore one viable alternative is to institutionalise internal policy competition and deepen internal democracy within the PAP, beyond just secret elections to a central committee or politburo.

Several very different and dominant Asian political parties — from those in Japan to China to Vietnam — already have intra-party competition through competing internal factions and cliques, overseen and endorsed by an informal cabal of elders. It can produce a reasonably sustainable succession process where competition allows the most capable and broadly popular leaders to emerge.

However, because this is largely informal, it is subject to back-room intrigue and horse-trading to the benefit of influential king-makers. It is also a competition over individuals, and not a competition of ideas.

An attempt to institutionalise a transparent internal competitive selection process not just for leadership roles but between party caucuses which represent different philosophical or policy tendencies, may be an innovative and sustainable way to combat complacency in long-ruling founding parties.

By itself however, internal party competition cannot ensure that a political elite will remain relevant to the needs of a changing population. On the contrary, civil society must be further empowered as a partner to strengthen the social contract, and also act as a check against inept or corrupt governance.

This involves nourishing civil society players with that lifeblood of robust discussion: freely available and largely unrestricted information. It is something I advocated in my final IPS-Nathan lecture, and I notice that we are steadily improving on that front. The government's statistics department is making more data available on its website as well as on the more interactive platform, data.gov.sg modelled on the American open data site, and when any points of controversy in public policy emerge, you can be sure you will find some issue-specific data on the site called "factually". The notion that the less information the public has equates to the less they can criticise, is a natural, universal, bureaucratic impulse which is slowly giving way to the realisation that wide and deep access to information is a key measure of participatory democracy.

Access to information enables the public to robustly debate and articulate ground-up responses to the pressing societal issues of the day. An information-rich society is all the more important since we have seen in the recent US presidential election, how social media can easily distort facts and even manufacture dis-information.

Our government was prescient to warn about the inherent flaws and anti-democratic dangers of unfettered social media, but the preservation of a social contract that might begin to fray cannot be achieved by an instinctive knee-jerk clampdown on social media, even if it were possible in the digital age.

The solution is not in more regulation and censorship, but in more citizen watchdogs monitoring falsehoods and pointing these out. Lies can only be destroyed by the sunlight of diverse and plentiful sources of the truth, and by civil society constantly building up its intellectual sinews to grapple with the arguments about current approaches in public policy and governance, as well as options for future.

In conclusion, 2065 is a destination for which the journey is fraught with uncertainties. The simplistic solution which traditional liberal democrats have held out — a pendulum form of democracy — is not necessarily the most desirable or the most likely scenario for Singapore. Yet the track record of continuously ruling founding parties has not been good. How the PAP can reinvent itself with the benefit of historical hindsight to ensure robust internal competition, and also truly engage civil society in genuine participatory democracy, will shape the future of our nation.

About the Contributors

Jeremy AU is the co-founder of Quad.sg, a non-partisan collective of individuals expanding the space for data-driven discourse and assisting in better collective decisions for Singapore's future. He was recognised by Forbes' "30 Under 30 Asia" for co-founding Conjunct Consulting, a social enterprise that empowers pro bono talent to strengthen organisations that deliver social good. Mr Au graduated from University of California, Berkeley, was a former Bain consultant, and at the time of writing, a candidate in the Master of Business Administration programme at the Harvard Business School.

Amanda CHONG is a lawyer with strong interests in criminal justice and public policy. She attended Cambridge University on a President's Scholarship and specialised in international human rights at Harvard Law School, where she developed an expertise in trafficking in persons and gender justice.

Ms Chong writes poetry during her lunch breaks. A winner of the Foyle Young Poets of the Year Award, her poetry has been engraved on the Marina Bay Helix Bridge and included in the Cambridge International GCSE syllabus. She is interested in exploring themes of gender and power in both her poetry and academic writing, which has been published in the *Harvard Journal of Law and Gender*. Her creative work has appeared in *Monocle*, *The Straits Times* and *Quarterly Literary Review Singapore*. Her first collection of poetry, *Professions*, was published in 2016.

Ms Chong also co-founded ReadAble, a non-profit organisation that runs weekly English literacy classes for children and migrant women in a low-income neighbourhood since 2014, with the aim of improving social mobility. She serves as web editor for poetry.sg, the first online database of Singapore poetry, complete with critical analyses and a multimedia archive.

Janadas DEVAN, Director of the Institute of Policy Studies, was educated at the National University of Singapore and Cornell University in the United States. He was a journalist, writing for *The Straits Times* and broadcasting for Radio Singapore International, before being appointed the Government's Chief of Communications at the Ministry of Communications and Information in 2012. He is now concurrently Deputy Secretary at the Prime Minister's Office.

HO Kwon Ping is Executive Chairman of Banyan Tree Holdings. Born in 1952, he was educated in Tunghai University, Taiwan; Stanford University, California and the University of Singapore. He worked as a broadcast and financial journalist and was the Economics Editor of the *Far Eastern Economic Review*. In 1994, after successfully rehabilitating an abandoned tin mine into Laguna Phuket, Asia's first integrated resort, he launched Banyan Tree Hotels & Resorts, which has now grown to more than 40 hotels and resorts, over 70 spas and over 80 retail galleries, and three golf courses. Currently, over 20 projects are being developed around the world.

Mr Ho has been recognised for his numerous significant contributions. Mr Ho was conferred an honorary doctorate by Johnson & Wales University (2000) and received the London Business School Entrepreneurship Award (2005). He was named CEO of the Year at the Singapore Corporate Awards (2008) and was the first Asian to receive the American Creativity Association Lifetime Achievement Award (2010) for his creativity and innovation. Mr Ho also received the CNBC Travel Business Leader Award in Asia Pacific (2012). He was awarded the Singapore Government's Meritorious Service Medal (2013) for his contribution in the founding of the Singapore Management University as Chairman. He also sits on the board of Diageo, a British multinational company. He was the Institute of Policy Studies' S R Nathan Fellow for the Study of Singapore in the 2014/15 academic year, and his five IPS-Nathan Lectures on policy issues have been compiled into a book titled *The Ocean in a Drop — Singapore: The Next Fifty Years* (2015).

About the Contributors

KHONG Cho-Oon is Chief Political Analyst in the Global Business Environment team, Shell International, based in London, with over 20 years' experience leading and advising on country scenario projects. Dr Khong advises on political trends and political risk for the Shell Group, and leads the external environment assessments for Shell's country reviews. He was actively involved in developing the 1995, 1998, 2001 and 2005 sets of Shell Global Scenarios, the 2008 Shell Energy Scenarios and the 2013 New Lens Scenarios.

Dr Khong is an active scenarios practitioner, using scenarios in futures thinking and working with a range of organisations in the private and public sectors. He is a member of the Brains Trust of the Evian Group, International Institute for Management Development, Lausanne; Academy Adjunct Faculty Member at Chatham House; and Associate Fellow of the Saïd Business School, University of Oxford, where he teaches as a core faculty member on the Oxford Scenarios Programme.

Gillian KOH is Deputy Director (Research) at the Institute of Policy Studies and Senior Research Fellow and Head of its Politics and Governance research cluster, which analyses electoral politics, the development of civil society, state-society relations, citizen engagement in Singapore. Dr Koh conducts surveys on Singaporeans' political attitudes, sense of identity, rootedness and resilience. She has published and co-published articles on civil society and political development in Singapore. She was co-editor of *State-Society Relations in Singapore* (2000); *Migration and Integration in Singapore: Policies and Practice* (2015); and *Civil Society and the State in Singapore* (2017). She was co-author of *Singapore Chronicles: Civil Society* (2016).

Joseph LIOW is Dean and Professor of Comparative and International Politics at the S. Rajaratnam School of International Studies, Nanyang Technological University, Singapore. He held the inaugural Lee Kuan Yew Chair in Southeast Asia Studies at the Brookings Institution, Washington DC, where he was also a Senior Fellow in the Foreign Policy Program. Professor Liow's research interests encompass Muslim politics and social movements in Southeast Asia and the international politics of the Asia-Pacific region.

Professor Liow is the author, co-author, or editor of 14 books. His recent single-authored books are *Religion and Nationalism in Southeast Asia* (Cambridge University Press, 2016) and *Dictionary of the Modern Politics of Southeast Asia*, fourth edition (Routledge, 2014). He has a forthcoming book, *Ambivalent Engagement: The United States and Regional Security in Southeast Asia After the Cold War*, scheduled for publication by Brookings Institution Press in 2017. His commentaries on international affairs have been published in *Foreign Affairs, Foreign Policy, National Interest*, and the *Wall Street Journal*. In addition to scholarship and analysis, Professor Liow has also consulted for a wide range of multinational corporations including Shell, BHP Billiton, Chevron, and Statoil. He is a graduate of the University of Wisconsin-Madison, Nanyang Technological University and the London School of Economics and Political Science.

Aaron MANIAM at the time of writing was a civil servant overseeing policy on manufacturing, services and tourism. He previously served as a diplomat from 2004 to 2008 (including at Singapore's Embassy in Washington DC); as the inaugural Head of the Singapore Government's newly-formed Centre for Strategic Futures from 2008 to 2011, and as Director of the Institute of Policy Development at the Civil Service College, which organises leadership training programmes for public sector talent.

In June 2012, Mr Maniam was conferred the Singapore Youth Award, the highest national honour for young people who exemplify excellence in their professional lives and community work, by the Prime Minister of Singapore. In March 2013, he was named by the World Economic Forum as one of 200 Young Global Leaders, selected from a worldwide pool. In May 2014, he was named a member of the "Purpose Economy Asia 100" by the United States-based firm Imperative, which identifies pioneers in purpose-driven management in the Asia-Pacific. A published poet, he won the National Arts Council's Golden Point Award in 2003. His first collection, *Morning at Memory's Border* was shortlisted for the Singapore Literature Prize in 2007. He is a trained facilitator of inter-religious dialogue and a Fellow of the Royal Society for the encouragement of Arts, Manufactures and Commerce (RSA).

About the Contributors

MARIAM Jaafar is a Partner and Managing Director at The Boston Consulting Group (BCG) Singapore. She is a core member of the Technology, Media and Telecommunications and Financial Services practices. Ms Mariam has worked with both public and private sector clients in the United States and Southeast Asia. Her recent focus has been on helping clients respond to and pursue opportunities from digital disruption. She also leads Wealth Management for BCG across Asia Pacific. Ms Mariam has served as Chief of Staff and Chief Operating Officer of Barclays Wealth Management Asia, Middle East and Africa. She started her career with Vertex Management, the venture capital arm of the Singapore Technologies group.

Ms Mariam holds a Master of Business Administration from the Harvard Business School as well as a Master and Bachelor of Science in Electrical Engineering (with Distinction) from Stanford University. She served on the Committee on the Future Economy and was Co-Chair of the Sub-Committee on the Future of Connectivity. She is a board member of the Government Technology Agency of Singapore (GovTech).

ONG Ye Kung was elected Member of Parliament for Sembawang Group Representation Constituency in September 2015, and appointed to the Cabinet of Singapore as the Acting Minister for Education (Higher Education and Skills) on 1 October 2015. He also held the concurrent appointment of Senior Minister of State for Defence. On 1 November 2016, he was promoted to Education Minister (Higher Education and Skills), and concurrently, Second Minister in the Ministry of Defence. Prior to his Cabinet appointment, he held the position of Director of Group Strategy at Keppel Corporation, overseeing long-term strategic planning of the Group's activities. Before joining Keppel Corporation, he was the Deputy Secretary-General of National Trades Union Congress, overseeing the Labour Movement's employment and employability programmes.

He also held various positions in government earlier. These include Chief Executive of Singapore Workforce Development Agency (WDA), during which he spearheaded many initiatives to build up the Continuing Education and Training infrastructure. He was Principal Private Secretary to Prime Minister Lee Hsien Loong from 2003 to 2005, and Press Secretary to Prime Minister Lee from 1997 to 2003. Mr Ong was also the Deputy

Chief Negotiator for the United States-Singapore Free Trade Agreement. Mr Ong graduated from the London School of Economics and Political Science (UK) with a Bachelor of Science (Econs, First Class Honours), and holds a Master of Business Administration from the International Institute for Management Development, Lausanne, Switzerland.

Pravin PRAKASH is an Associate Research Fellow with the Social Resilience Programme at the Centre of Excellence for National Security within the S. Rajaratnam School of International Studies, Nanyang Technological University. He received his Master of Social Sciences in Political Science (with distinction) and his Bachelor of Social Sciences with honours in Political Science from the National University of Singapore (NUS).

Pravin has penned several commentaries and articles on meritocracy, multiculturalism, identity politics, civil society and local politics on various platforms. He has also delivered lectures and tutored modules with the Political Science and South Asian Studies departments at NUS. His research interests include state-society relations, ethno-nationalism, secularism, communal relations, immigration and the experiences of diasporic communities.

Debbie SOON is a Research Associate at the Institute of Policy Studies (IPS) of the National University of Singapore. Her research interests are in the study of political identities, ideologies, and political communication. Her published work includes co-authored chapters on migration, identity, and civil society issues. She received her Master's degree in Sociology from the University of Essex, UK.

THANG Leng Leng is Deputy Director of the Centre for Family and Population Research at the National University of Singapore. She is a socio-cultural anthropologist with research interests in the areas of ageing, intergenerational approaches and relationships, gender and family. She publishes widely in her areas of expertise with a focus on Asia, especially Japan and Singapore. Associate Professor Thang is also active in community service, currently serving on the boards of Fei Yue Family Service Centre (chair), Fei Yue Community Services, Centre for Seniors and the council of Gerontological Society of Singapore. She is a member of the Families for Life Council, which promotes strong families. Associate Professor Thang advocates for intergenerational approaches in the community and is often consulted on intergenerational programmes and relationship issues.

Internationally, she is co-editor-in-chief of the *Journal of Intergenerational Relationships* (Taylor and Francis, USA) and vice-chair of the International Consortium for Intergenerational Programs. Besides heading the Department of Japanese Studies at the Faculty of Arts and Social Sciences, she is also Honorary Fellow with the College of Alice and Peter Tan, National University of Singapore.

Norman VASU is Senior Fellow, Coordinator of the Social Resilience Programme and Deputy Head of the Centre of Excellence for National Security at the S. Rajaratnam School of International Studies, Nanyang Technological University. He is the author of *How Diasporic Peoples Maintain Their Identity in Multicultural Societies: Chinese, Africans, and Jews* (2008); editor of *Social Resilience in Singapore: Reflections from the London Bombings* (2007); co-editor of *Nations, National Narratives and Communities in the Asia Pacific* (2014) as well as *Immigration in Singapore* (2015).

Dr Vasu has published and co-published academic articles and book chapters on narratives of governance, policies of multiculturalism, gender and politics, and national security and resilience. His research interests include communal relations, narratives of governance, citizenship, immigration and national security.

WANG Gungwu is University Professor at the National University of Singapore (NUS) and Emeritus Professor at the Australian National University (ANU). He is Chairman of the Institute of Southeast Asian Studies-Yusof Ishak Institute; and of the East Asian Institute. He was Chairman of the Lee Kuan Yew School of Public Policy at NUS from 2004 to 2016.

His recent books in English include *Diasporic Chinese Ventures: The Life and Work of Wang Gungwu* (2004); *Renewal: The Chinese State and the New Global History* (2013); and *Another China Cycle: Committing to Reform* (2014). His dialogues on world history were edited by Ooi Kee Beng and published as *The Eurasian Core and its Edges* (2015).

Professor Wang received his Bachelor and Master of Arts from the University of Malaya in Singapore, and his doctoral degree at the University of London. He was Professor of History at the University of Malaya; Professor of Far Eastern History and Director of the Research School of Pacific Studies at ANU. From 1986 to 1995, he was Vice-Chancellor of the University of Hong Kong. In Singapore, he was Director of the East Asian Institute at the NUS from 1997 to 2007.

www.ingramcontent.com/pod-product-compliance
Lightning Source LLC
Chambersburg PA
CBHW052134010526
44113CB00036B/2173